*Foreign
and Other
Affairs*

Foreign and Other Affairs

JOHN PATON DAVIES, Jr.

W · W · NORTON & COMPANY · INC ·

New York

For

P.G.D.

A.H.D.

P.F.D.

J.G.D.

S.M.D.

J.V.D.

D.E.D.

M.M.D.

Contents

The Sleepwalker   11

Why Ouagadougou?   15

Roughshod over Slipshod   39

Imbalance of Terror   63

Paul Bunyan and the United Nations   79

Sharper Than a Serpent's Tooth   97

The Other Cold War   117

Europa and the Bull in the China Shop   141

Disgraceful and Ruinous Mutability?   163

Above All Zeal   183

In Search of Monsters   201

Foreign
and Other
Affairs

The Sleepwalker

*A*s in a deep and troubled sleep, wrapped in exalted yet fearful dreams, American foreign policy walked into the decade of the 1960's.

The world of actuality lay round about, scarcely perceived. What was immediate, urgent, and absorbing was the subjective drama in a world of the subconscious. The dreams demanded of the sleepwalker desperate exertions to save himself and distant strangers from an interminable succession of crises near and far.

In only two major respects did the conduct of American foreign affairs depart from somnambulism and relate to the realities of the international environment.

Most important was the maintenance and bettering of American military superiority over the Soviet Union. This accomplishment was probably definitive in changing the course of the cold war to our favor. The other, the fruition of a process begun even earlier, was the contribution of the United States to the recovery of Western Europe and Japan.

Both had been master strokes. They were, it should be repeated, close to reality. The creation of novel and supreme military power was a scientific-technological–production undertaking in the American tradition suited to the American genius and accomplished within the conscious and familiar setting of the American military-economic complex.

The assistance to Western Europe's and Japan's renaissance was also close to reality. The Europeans and the Japanese had the will, wit, skill, and discipline to use American aid effectively.

The other major themes of American foreign policy were sleepwalking. The Grand Design for a vaguely united Europe in partnership with the United States was one. The making over of Latin America, its de-Latinization through the Alliance for Progress, was another.

Then there was the nightmare of our rigidly pushing against the spectral monolith of international communism lest it crash down upon us, crush and bury us beneath a solid bulk that was not.

In darkness through the sultry, sluggish villages of Southeast Asia we wandered, our eyes open, but somehow alone with our dream, talking in our sleep, anxiously summoning the fatalistic to challenge their fate, to join battle with that which they did not know or, knowing, feared, did not care about, or even admired.

And there is still the haunted quest for peace and justice through the tiered halls of the United Nations, with doors opening, shutting, and swinging back and forth in the eerie high winds of rhetoric.

These and other dreams emerged out of emotional disturbance—a pervasive anxiety and a sense of mission. The apprehension, an unsettling new experience for Americans, sprang from a sudden public awareness in the late forties of the Soviet menace, extending from subversion to nuclear assault.

The sense of national mission was a figment of the New Frontier. In response to the ideological and revolutionary challenge of the Communists, the Kennedy administration proclaimed our responsibility to lead a revolution based on the principles clarioned in the Declaration of Independence, a great world revolution, a revolution so flexible that it answers the needs of all countries, races, and cultures. This moral militancy of the federal government bore little relation to realities at home or abroad.

It was an upsetting combination. Anxiety interacted with vaulting but frustrated moral compulsions. The result was that American diplomacy stumbled as it walked out its dreams.

In order to bring a sleepwalker out of his trance, he must be awakened. If not thoroughly roused, if soothed by official cant and buncombe, the dream returns and the somnambulist is soon again roaming about, nearly oblivious to his real environment, absorbed in his private chimera.

The surest awakening is gradual but insistent. And for a whole society—because the affliction goes deeper than the Kennedy-Johnson administrations—the coming to terms with reality is a slow, unwelcome process.

There is no pretense that this series of commentaries is a prescription for a sudden return to reality. Rather, it is a collection of random but related observations of an unfrocked diplomat on some key issues affecting American foreign relations.

Foreign and Other Affairs

The perspective is from afar—from a carpentry shop at the foot of the Andes—lending, if not enchantment, some measure of objectivity to an underlying affection.

The angle of vision lies between the radical right and the radical left, holding as best it can to the radical center.

Why Ouagadougou?

*T*he committee of the House of Representatives charged with passing on the foreign-aid program was in session. It was July 9, 1962. A portion of the deliberations as preserved in *The Congressional Record* reads thusly:

MR. KYL.   Perhaps some of these things are out of order, but there is one matter I want to ask about. Is the Government going to spend $635,000 for buildings in Ouagadougou to house 15 Americans?

MR. GROSS.   What is that?

MR. KYL.   Ouagadougou.

MR. GROSS.   Where is that?

MR. KYL.   On the upper Volta.

MR. GROSS.   What?

MR. KYL.   On the upper Volta.

MR. GROSS.   Volta or Volga? . . .

MRS. BOLTON.   I am told by one of the men who knows Africa rather well that it is on the lower Volta, not the upper Volta; and it is not in this bill at all. I hope we will not waste any time on things outside of this bill . . .

MR. GROSS.   I wonder if the $3 million item for air conditioning a yacht for Haile Selassie is in this bill, or was it provided for in the bill last year?

MR. KYL. Mr. Chairman, will the gentleman yield?

MR. GROSS. I yield.

MR. KYL. Perhaps the gentleman will permit one further reference. It is to this matter of the taxpayers having to spend $256,000 on a 122-day tour to some place by one Joey Adams and about some other uncomplimentary behavior of those who went with him on this particular tour. Was this part of the program in the bill?

MR. GROSS. I yield to someone else to answer the gentleman.

MRS. BOLTON. If the gentleman will yield, Mr. Chairman, this also is no part of this bill.

One may sympathize with everyone concerned in these proceedings. But meanwhile Ouagadougou and the rest of the underdeveloped third of the world had their problems, too. In microcosm, a segment of them might look something like this.

Malaria had for centuries been endemic, weakening and killing the people in parts of the countryside. The country could be in Asia, Africa, or Latin America. A malarial eradication unit, armed with insecticides, went to work in the region. The anopheline mosquito was brought under control. A mobile public-health clinic treated and instructed those with the disease.

Narrowing the focus, a pregnant peasant woman, ill with malaria, survived to bear a son—and many children thereafter. The boy who otherwise would not have been, thanks again to insecticides and antibiotics, lived through a hungry childhood. He got the equivalent of a second-grade education and worked his father's tiny plot of land with the rest of the family. But none of them had enough to eat.

So at seventeen he rode a truck to the metropolis—it could be Calcutta, or Cairo, or Caracas—to look for work with machines at a wage fabulous to village ears. He would help to support those at home.

He shared a mud-floored one-room shack with his uncle, who had abandoned his wife and children in the village to work in a paint factory. Also sharing the shanty were his uncle's tubercular common-law wife, acquired in the metropolis, and her two small daughters by a previous alliance. The woman took medicine irregularly and could not afford the rest necessary for a cure.

After running up six weeks of debts to his uncle for rent and food, the youth got a job as cleaner in a garage specializing in repair by cannibalization of defunct or stolen cars. His fabulous wage covered his current keep by his uncle but was not enough to reduce his debt, much less to send money back home.

His leisure? Shyly gawking in the streets of the big city. But this did not last long. He quickly became one of the shanty settlement wise guys. The compulsions and restraints of the village, themselves disintegrating, were made light of. He was one of a bored, shiftless gang of youths without the means or the self-disciplined determination to get an education, hostile to and envious of those in fine houses, and without hope that he might himself someday achieve such status. Yet he had no longing to return to the total stagnation of the village.

By young manhood he had, through observation and practice, become a junior mechanic. His wage had risen, but so had prices with inflation. And so had his expenses, for he had brought to live with him in his uncle's shack, now expanded by a second lean-to room, a girl who worked in a textile factory and by whom he sired two or three children—he was not sure about the second.

His uncle's family had grown by one; it would have been three, but one baby died of tuberculosis and another of an overdose of a new drug administered at a public-health clinic. He quietly moved to bachelor diggings in another part of town when his uncle suddenly died of pneumonia contracted when the paint factory, in a modernization program, installed air conditioning.

A brother and sister came to the metropolis. Life on the land had become harder. An agrarian reform, mismanaged by big bureaucrats in the metropolis and a petty grafter in the village, had provided the family with two additional acres three miles from its old plot, but nothing with which to get started on the new land.

By the time the brother and sister arrived, he had living with him a girl who helped sell vegetables in the main market. The four shared a room in a tenement. They were all on slim rations for weeks, until the sister got a job in a shoe factory and the younger brother, in desperation, mugged a tourist, seeking people-to-people contacts, for a hundred and fifty dollars. The policeman who caught him allowed him to keep ten, after which each went his independent way, sensibly avoiding the fuss of courts and jails, both of which were overcrowded.

The fraternal congestion was relieved when the sister was taken in marriage, for her youth and beauty, by a middle-aged foreman in the shoe factory. He was a slogan-bearer and cheerleader among the labor phalanxes of the dominant political movement. After ten years in a two- then three-room model apartment with a radio then a TV set, she departed this life as a result of complications arising out of obesity, leaving six offspring.

In the meantime the younger brother had drifted from menial job to unemployment to unskilled job to unemployment. Insecure, embittered, and willful, he joined an underground revolutionary movement against the revolution of the established revolutionary movement. He had the creed repetitiously in mind but was a little fuzzy on the reasoning, which itself shared this attribute. Nevertheless the cause demanded much of him, he found comradeship, and he felt purposeful and important. Although the educated middle-class leaders of the movement were distant and condescending in their treatment of him and other lower-class comrades, he was not troubled, for he acknowledged revolutionary privilege when he saw it. Before long the secret police picked him up in his brother's room. He kept his secrets and was locked up for five years.

It also went hard with the older brother. He was grilled by the police and then let go, successively by the investigators and the nervous manager of the garage. For eight months he was jobless and was supported, together with his two children, by the provisional spare-time streetwalking of their mother. The children survived on Food for Peace lunches at school.

He was finally taken on as a cleaner, credentials waived, in a crash program to stamp out malaria in the region from whence he had come. For fifteen years the children of the area had been born, lived, and themselves begun to reproduce without exposure to natural immunization. The anopheline mosquito had been controlled but not eradicated. There had been a letup in the spraying because two careless sprayers had died of leukemia from the insecticide. The mosquitoes then reappeared, and with them, malaria recurred, but now in epidemic form, among the teeming, vulnerable new generation.

Not all died from the epidemic—only those already suffering from acute malnutrition. A team of doctors and nurses with drugs flown from the United States stamped out the epidemic. A new eradication unit, pulled up to snuff by the World Health Organization, brought the mosquitoes under control. The insecticidal-pharmaceutical ecology was reestablished. Man again lived and bred beyond his productive performance.

As the one and a half billion people in the underdeveloped countries this side of the Iron Curtain flounder in the slough of more and ever more of themselves—hungry, displaced, agglomerated, demoralized, and finally desperate or despairing—we of the industrialized west and north, one-third their number, are producing ever more food and things. The average annual per capita income in the underdeveloped countries is estimated at about $100. The average American spends more than $100 per year on recreation and some $480 on food and tobacco. These are static measures of the gap.

A dynamic and broader measure is one of investment rate.

The industrial west and north is making a per capita investment, out of savings, roughly equal to the total per capita income of the underdeveloped countries. Thus the advanced countries are becoming richer as the backward ones tread the water of poverty.

The American people are vaguely aware of this chasm between them and the majority of people in the world, and it troubles them. It does not seem right. The world should not be part rich and part poor, part overfed and part underfed.

This uneasiness of conscience is one of the reasons that the American people have gone along with their government's foreign-aid program. And it is one of the reasons advanced by the government for such assistance to foreign countries.

The Senate's Foreign Relations Committee stated in 1961:

> Foreign aid is both an unavoidable responsibility and a central instrument of our foreign policy. It is dictated by the hard logic of the cold war and by a moral responsibility resulting from poverty, hunger, disease, ignorance, feudalism, strife, revolution, chronic instability and life without hope.

This creed was restated and adopted by the Secretary of State in presenting the case for foreign aid in 1962.

Expanding the theme of the government's moral responsibility, the Counselor of the State Department in 1963 declared that it is "true that the richer nations have . . . basic impulses of religion, ethics, and humanity, to help the less advanced peoples." President Kennedy, in November, 1963, speaking of the government's foreign-aid program, referred to "our obligations to our fellow man—obligations that stem from our wealth and strength, from our devotion to freedom and from our membership in the family of man."

This is a delicate issue—do governments have moral, religious, ethical and humanitarian obligations to foreigners? Does wealth or strength impose such obligations on national states? Are governments even constitutionally capable of assuming such responsibilities, short of being explicitly charged with them by their own citizenry and the recipient foreigners?

As individuals we can feel a moral, religious, ethical, or humanitarian duty to others, no matter where they are. We can voluntarily join together with those of like mind to form private associations to satisfy the individual conscience and carry out the collective will—the Red Cross, missionary societies, CARE, HOPE, Foster Parents, and a host of others. The gift is freely given, clear in intent, uninvolved with national prestige, national interest, or the waging of cold wars.

The fixed responsibilities of a government, however, are limited to its own citizenry. Venturesome responsibilities with regard to other peoples are deliberately assumed and by no means unavoidable. Even the extent of the moral obligations of a government to its own people is debatable, as witness medicare. Far more questionable is the assumption of moral responsibility for aliens, and then taxing one's own citizenry in satisfaction of that moral urge.

Governments are not notably equipped to undertake moral judgments outside the dictates of national law. Our national policy enmeshes itself in a tangle of motives when it is dictated by moral considerations regarding foreigners, as evaluated and defined by politicians and bureaucrats. Mixing policy and morality usually leads to self-righteousness, exaggerated expectations, offended sensibilities, moral recriminations, and a train of emotional reactions needlessly befogging and complicating relations between states, often without accomplishing the ends sought. It is not even certain that the assistance to others will be regarded by the recipients as a moral act.

Some foreigners will say, as they now do, that foreign aid is an emasculation, that it makes them dependent. "Buy our raw materials at a decent price and you can keep your aid and we our self-respect." "We would prefer to work out our destiny in our own way without having to accept charity or humiliating conditions." "Foreign aid is immoral."

A qualified witness on this score, Prime Minister Nehru, was quoted on September 27, 1961, as observing: "People may think that you can do everything with money." Criticizing "the mentality of the receiver of the dole and the giver of the dole," Mr. Nehru noted: "That mentality is not good for either party and it makes people rather indolent and waiting for things to happen, for others to do them."

The case for foreign aid by our government is on firmer ground when it is related only to the national interest of the United States.

There are three bases for foreign aid related to national interest. One is—and this is the least fuzzily defined—assistance that strengthens strategically critical positions in the cold war. Assistance to Korea or Berlin is clearly in that category.

A second basis given for assistance to foreigners is that it will make them economically viable in the modern world, politically decent and upright, loyal adherents to the UN Charter, and, in sum, immune to communist subversion. Obviously this is a vaguely expansive category. Within its undefined limits belongs, for instance, the Alliance for Progress.

A third reason for foreign aid is promotion of American business by, in effect, government subsidy. In 1963, some 90 per cent of our aid commitments was used for the purchase of American goods and services. Production of foreign-assistance exports, furthermore, employed more than half a million American workers.

With regard to strengthening strategically critical areas, there can be no doubt that the assistance granted under the Marshall Plan was justified in American strategic interest. Not to have underwritten the recovery of Western Europe could well have resulted in a crucial Soviet victory early in the cold war. The aid to Greece, Turkey, Iran, and Japan likewise forestalled Soviet gains in areas of strategic importance.

Aid to Yugoslavia was strategically sound, even though to a Marxist regime, because it contributed to disunity in and a weakening of the Soviet power complex. To a lesser degree the same was true of help to Poland.

In South Vietnam and Laos, American aid helped stave off communist takeover, but the price was high for inconclusive results. Waste, misuse, and misgovernment in these countries sapped the effectiveness of American assistance.

The American struggle against communism both in vital

strategic areas and in less critical ones has sometimes been criticized by foreigners as a damaging influence in the world. A case can be made that quite the contrary is so. The cold war has been one of the most creative forces in history. Had it not been for the threat of Soviet aggression it is doubtful that we would have spent seventy billion dollars in economic assistance, helping to produce the miracles of the new Europe and the new Japan, building dams, roads, and schools in unexpected places, raising food production, sanitizing the unsanitary, and tutoring the untutored. More directly attributable to the stimulus of the communist threat is the additional thirty billion that we have spent on military supplies to and the training and maintenance of foreigners.

The Soviet Union, which started the cold war as a predatory enterprise, has ironically been forced by our burst of benefaction into painful competition in doing good. Soviet aid has ranged from a sports stadium for the Indonesians to snowplows for those dwelling in the African rain forest. Soviet and other communist assistance to underdeveloped countries is valued at more than eight billion dollars.

Even the Red Chinese in their cold war within the cold war against the Russians have deprived their famished, bedraggled masses to the benefit of faraway strangers in less frightful plight.

It therefore ill becomes those who have benefited from aid to protest against the cold war. The strain, nervous and financial, has been upon the contestants. To those who regard themselves as the victimized bystanders have gone the spoils.

Among the most articulate of those who so regard them-

selves are many of the countries to whom we give aid with
the hope that they will modernize their economies and reform their societies and thereby immunize themselves against
communism. Our government acknowledges that these trans-
formations can be accomplished only if the governments
and influential private elements in the nations concerned
are determined to put through the changes.

Testifying before the Senate Foreign Relations Committee on the Foreign Assistance Act of 1962, the Secretary
of State, Mr. Rusk, declared that

> the fundamental and indispensable requirement for the
> development of a nation is the determination of its own
> government and people to move forward; . . . their ef-
> forts must in all cases include mobilization of national
> resources—economic, financial, and human; . . . they
> must include . . . reforms in taxation, in landholdings,
> in housing, and the broadening and improvement of edu-
> cational opportunities. We must constantly bear in mind
> that our goal is not just economic development. It is
> equally and concurrently to increase social justice which
> will secure the benefits of progress . . .

This is a mighty tall order for most underdeveloped countries. But on into 1964, at least, Washington did not flinch
from imposing these requirements, albeit erratically. We
had every right to make our help depend on performance,
for the resources offered were our own and it was proper
that we lay down what seemed to us reasonable conditions
for the effective use of our aid.

This was not, however, the immediate issue. The first
issue was—did Washington's conditions make sense? Was
it realistic to demand that economic development and social

reform progress "equally and concurrently" or, as in certain Latin-American cases, that "social justice" come first?

The usual human experience has been that social improvements follow economic advances. The reason is that social benefits—take universal primary education as a starter—are beyond the resources of a backward society. Wealth must be generated or otherwise acquired in order to provide for these advantages.

The cost has been high for those societies that have done it on their own. Britain, Japan, and the Soviet Union are three disparate cases. About the only thing that they had in common was that they were in the same general latitude. Yet their patterns of growth had certain things in common.

A small minority decided instinctively or by plan to industrialize and expand the economy. They kept control of the process in their own hands. They siphoned off a small fraction of the increase for their personal benefit. The bulk of it was reinvested. None was distributed to improve the life of the workers. To the contrary, generations of workers and peasants were sacrificed to the national growth process. But it worked.

And now they are advanced nations. While the Soviet Union, as a totalitarian state, can hardly be said to dispense social justice, the Kremlin has perforce taken the first steps away from terror on a course pointing toward either a humane relationship with its subjects or a catastrophic attempt to return to Stalinism, for there can now be no workable turning back.

Washington has produced the new prescription—do it without agony and delay; do it with contributions—from the United States and other advanced countries. Maybe this will work. We do not know. It has never been tried before. The post-World War II European and Japanese recovery performances have little relation, of course, to the brute creative effort required of the backward nations.

Perhaps the first thing to be said is that the great majority of the underdeveloped countries have little in common but their indigence and their latitude. Most lie between the Tropics of Cancer and Capricorn. Most are the hot countries.

Although God created all men equal, he did not so create all physical enivronments. This is a subject skittishly explored and seldom touched upon, but it is a reality that heat, humidity or extreme aridity, and slight variations in temperature do not always have beneficial effects on subhuman animal life (except insects and predatory beasts), man himself, and machinery. The environment in this zone does not, in short, contribute to a high factor of efficiency.

The second consideration is the time factor. Time is as short as tempers in the underdeveloped countries and patience in the advanced ones. No one is willing to go through the long time phase, even painlessly, that it took Britain, Japan, or the U.S.S.R. This is because of what is called the revolution of rising expectations or demands. The clamor is for instant solutions—on the one side for immediate satisfaction of wants, on the other for quick relief from the aid burden.

A third basic consideration in the underdeveloped countries is the ratio of growth between production and population. The productive performance in the early sixties was not impressive. The multiplication of population was alarming. Unless the growth of production is steadily well ahead of the growth of population, either disaster or enormously increased aid lies ahead.

The New Frontier mystique was not, however, daunted by this combination of ominous circumstances. Imbued with the faith that has stood us in such good stead in our own history that all things are possible, Washington professed to believe that the transformation of the underdeveloped part of the world through American capital and technical assistance plus self-reform by the recipients was a feasible proposition.

In theory, a good case was made that this was so. Schematically it went something like this.

Develop the industrial base, remembering that one of its main functions is to stimulate and supply rural growth. Develop agriculture to (1) feed the growing population, (2) generate raw materials for industry and to earn foreign exchange, and (3) provide an expanding market for domestic industry and a source of increasing tax revenues. Develop and reform public administration to plan, coordinate, and guide the growth process, while providing the education, technical services, and infrastructure of public facilities, all essential to progress.

It is not necessary here to go into the intricate interaction of the multitude of institutions and individuals, private and governmental, national and international, that should function relatively smoothly to produce national growth. It is possible to skip all this and go to the crucial factor—the human element. In practice, this is where the case for aid to the underdeveloped is most fallible.

Remembering that Washington wanted the development to proceed without the repressions characteristic of the early stages of British and Japanese modernization, there should then be collaboration between and self-restraint and self-sacrifice on the part of the various elements in the society, all working toward the goal of national growth. Any such expectation was, of course, illusory in the ferment and inertia characteristic of most underdeveloped societies.

Even had there been a basic social harmony of purpose, there remained the problem of the competence and vigor, not to mention integrity, of the system of public administration. Many of the leading figures in the governments of backward countries are themselves intelligent, well-educated, vigorous, and honest. In general, the same cannot be said of their subordinates, through whom they must operate and upon whom they are dependent. And without a reasonably competent public administration, foreign assistance is at best wasteful and at worst futile or even directly damaging to us.

It was these human inadequacies that provoked the New Frontiersmen into inciting reform. The Kennedy administration in 1961 felt under pressure to produce prompt, dramatic results with aid. It wanted to make a better record than the Eisenhower administration in fending off communism. Reinforcing its own impatience was the mounting popular demand in the underdeveloped countries for the ready-made fruits of developed status. The prospects for progress were, however, prejudiced in many underdeveloped countries by certain vested interests and by incompetence.

Obviously, thought the New Frontiersmen, the only thing to do to get an urgent solution, short of physical take-over by us rather than the communists, was to demand drastic, thoroughgoing reform.

In many countries this amounted to inciting revolution. The reforms that we asked seemed for most of the lagging nations disruptive of either a long-established status quo or a newly formed oligarchy. Only to enforce the tax laws already on the books, for example, would have caused in many countries an economic upheaval and social chaos. The influential elements in these countries were therefore unreceptive to Washington's finger-wagging about their economic and social ethics. Either the old-line combinations that held power or the newly forming ones would have resisted with violence, if necessary, changes threatening the prerogatives and power of the native establishment, whether pseudo-capitalist or "socialist."

These are normal human attitudes and behavior. What was odd was the widespread American assumption that those enjoying privilege and authority would be good sports and yield both at our behest. Reforms of the magnitude and at the pace that we proposed, if the past is a guide, can be accomplished only through a bloody social revolution, as in Mexico, or imposition of authoritarianism, as in Egypt.

The question arises: were the New Frontiersmen aware of what they were up to? To a degree, yes. We all rather fancy ourselves as old-grad revolutionaries. As we revolted against paying taxes, so if it takes a revolution to make "oligarchs" pay their taxes and divide up those big plantations, let the revolutions rip.

The catch is that the tidy, constructive ends we wish to see achieved are not predictably served by violent, erratic means over which control is easily lost, quite possibly to our adversaries. We do not have the wisdom, temperament, discretion, or self-discipline to play around with other people's social systems. We should face the fact that we are a middle-aged, conservative society, reluctant to make drastic adjustments to the revolutionary impact of science and technology on our own social system, and that our gentry-led revolution is remote in time and kind from that which goes on nowadays in the underdeveloped countries.

Our showiest social engineering has been the project for hemispheric uplift, *La Alianza para el Progreso*. It originated in apprehension, the mood most productive of aid programs. We correctly feared that Castroism might spread to other parts of Latin America. To counter this, the Latin-American governments had to develop, in our opinion, a competing revolutionary appeal. This meant radical reforms for most of them, transforming their countries economically, socially, and politically.

With ardor and innocence, the New Frontiersmen promoted the *Alianza*, giving it the hard sell. This was during the first year of the Kennedy administration when the newcomers were, as is the established practice, fomenting programs and slogans that would effervesce a bouquet of greatness.

The *Alianza* fit the need. It had the indispensable quality of bigness: a score of countries and a hundred billion dollars over a decade. Here was vision, thinking big. It had the excitement of action, getting more than the United States moving, getting an extra continent and a half moving. For the many who felt an obligation to improve others, there was the promise of slashing reforms, the role of vicarious revolutionaries. The *Alianza* also had the essential entwined ingredients of heart and conflict. It was good-neighborly cooperation against communist aggression.

The *Alianza* had a flaw. It was inoperable. At least, it could not work as the New Frontiersmen conceived it in 1961.

It was inoperable because it was grandiose, unmanageable on the scale presented. It was also blatantly hostile to the propertied classes and to the military who, with few exceptions and in varying combinations, rule Latin America. They were the ones marked for our reform schooling. These power elements were unsympathetic to the bumptious schemes out of Washington for their downfall. They had, it should be noted, the only organization and talent promptly available to attempt a huge crash program like the *Alianza*.

For our Latin friends the *Alianza* idea took a little getting used to—it was such a sudden new interest and emotion pulsing at them out of the north. They were familiar with and understood gringo moneymaking interest in them and Yanqui military intervention. They had become accustomed to subsequent gringo good-neighborliness, followed by Point Four technical help.

Then suddenly in 1961 the Yanquis proposed that over a decade they would put up twenty billion dollars for economic and social development if the Latins would put up 80 billion and turn everything upside down in their countries. And all of this thanks to the bearded one in Havana.

Adjusting themselves to these rare circumstances, the Latins at Punta del Este acceded to the idea of two billion dollars per year from abroad and with us issued a Declaration to the Peoples of America, a charter some sixteen times the length of the Atlantic Charter, and a train of sixteen resolutions. These eloquent expressions of elevated intent pretty much took care of, in the Latin mind, the need to do anything about reforms for a year or so. And for the New Frontiersmen, the pledge of Punta del Este became a major public-relations production.

By 1963 the buck fever of a new administration had subsided somewhat. Washington began to catch on to the fact that while it is difficult to save people from others, it is well nigh impossible to save them from themselves.

The *Alianza* dragged. No wave of reforms swept the hemisphere below the Rio Grande. And to the Kennedy administration's irritation, the Latins persisted in being themselves. When military coups d'état, traditional as fiestas in Latin America, occurred in a number of countries, Washington cracked down on some of the resulting juntas, apparently accepted others, but sounded off about all of them —and any that might be contemplated. It was an erratic performance, inspiring neither admiration nor awe. Worst of all, it was ineffectual, a defiance of diplomacy as the art of the possible.

The result of Washington's public feuds with the military and those commanding capital resources in Latin America was to encourage the demagogues. This meant, inevitably, febrile economic nationalism, inflation, and the flight of domestic capital from the consequent instability and reluctance of foreign capital to invest. As the *Alianza* counted heavily on private investments to contribute to the growth process, the administration had deftly, but apparently without thinking what it was doing, stabbed its favorite offspring in a vital part.

Can any useful conclusions be drawn about our government's aid operation not only in Latin America but also in Asia and Africa?

It may be worth recognizing that the transition of a country from underdeveloped to developed is a growth process. This process in a social organism is even slower (perhaps three generations), no less complicated, and more painful than in a single human organism. Trying to rush growth beyond the limits of organic tolerance, as we are doing with others in a Decade of Progress, is a mistake made by overanxious parents, the unwitting, or the heedless.

We should therefore reconcile ourselves to the inevitability of disorderly progress, of many wracking social revolutions, even of long inability to progress, lapsing into chaos. These things will happen no matter how much cash and ingenuity we put up. They are no cause for self-reproach. They are inescapably in the nature of the transition.

There is obviously a need for re-evaluation, including costing, of the foreign-aid program. The need goes beyond the executive branch, which cannot begin to function intelligently in these matters unless the Congress, too, has a rational grasp of the matter. And it goes beyond the Congress to the people, whose understandable confusion over what goes on deserves to be cleared up.

The primitive first question should, of course, test the object of the aid exercise. How would our national-security interest be affected were all the underdeveloped countries "lost" to communism? The answer to this would turn largely on how much their take-over by Communists would add to —or cost—Soviet or Chinese power. For of themselves, the backward countries are of less security significance to us.

There is probably no clear-cut answer to this question. But, whatever it may be, it will not conform to the horrendous specter of the 1950s—a regimental mass of Asians, Africans, and Latins obediently descending upon us at Moscow's command.

The next basic question is do aid and the stage of development really affect very much the vulnerability of a country to communism. In 1958, Cuba, the Dominican Republic, and Paraguay were ruled by military dictators. Cuba was the most developed of the three and had received the most American aid. It fell to communism. Trujillo was overthrown but by non-Communists. And Stroessner continued to rule Paraguay, the most backward of the three. Furthermore, Paraguay, which Washington kept on short aid rations because Stroessner was a military dictator, was the only nation in South America without a troublesome communist problem.

Upon reflection we may conclude that in underdeveloped societies the key factor in blocking communist take-overs is not economic or social but political. That is to say, it is an ability and will to govern. There are few underdeveloped regimes with this capacity.

Whatever basic conclusions might emerge from a reappraisal of the foreign-assistance program, it seems evident now that governmental aid should be greatly reduced. Those nations that have attained the level of developed countries should need no more American help. Some states, strategically not vital to our security, that are wastrels should not receive aid.

The nations of critical strategic importance to our security, let us recognize, have us blackmailed. So long as the national-security concern is valid, we have to support them if they need aid, even when they do not deserve it. Assistance to them, on a basis of our estimate of their need, should probably be kept on a bilateral, government-to-government basis.

Aid to the rest of the underdeveloped world should, for the self-respect of all concerned, be phased out of the American government. Capital assistance, in general, belongs back in the private sector and with the World Bank, the International Development Association, the Inter-American Development Bank, and other similar organizations.

Technical assistance, the provision of scientific and technological advice, carries quite a different connotation from that of capital assistance. Where asked for and used by an underdeveloped country, it can be supplied by the government, but it need not be on the expansive scale that it now is. And technological assistance, too, should in the main be phased over to nongovernmental organizations such as learned institutions.

Finally, needing no huge appropriations nor battalions of bureaucrats, is international trade. This has been an area of relative neglect. What is needed here is the lowering of trade barriers and the stabilization of commodity prices. With these, the underdeveloped countries can begin to pay their own way, moving at their own pace in their own fashion—a wholesome thing for them, and a wholesome thing for us.

Roughshod
over Slipshod

*C*olonel Briceño led the assault upon the Palace. He was one of the Peruvian Army officers trained in the United States to quell rebellions against the government.

His Sherman tanks and Rangers (garbed like their American prototypes in splotchy jungle camouflage) roared through predawn Lima into the Plaza de Armas in front of the Presidential Palace. It was shortly after 3 A.M. on July 18, 1962, when the Colonel, speaking over a public-address system for the generals and admirals behind the scenes, called upon the Palace to surrender in two minutes or suffer the consequences.

As is often the case when one group works itself up to do great violence on another, there came a breakdown in communication—the Colonel's loudspeaker gave forth but fitfully because, it was said, of the damp night air. Furthermore the President and his supporters, while conscious of the hullabaloo in the plaza and its general portent, were in the residential quarters at the rear of the Palace and so did not hear even that part of the Colonel's ultimatum that was sputtering in the square.

Earlier, while awaiting the arrival of the assault force, they had resolved to resist. Happily, good sense had subsequently prevailed so that they and the relieved Palace guard, the Hussars of Junin, were disposed to yield to superior force.

Receiving no response to his ultimatum, Colonel Briceño proceeded with equal good sense. He extended the presidential doom with a second ultimatum. Still getting no reaction to his repeated warning, instead of blasting the Palace with his tank artillery, he ordered one of the Shermans to nose open a Palace gate. The Colonel and his Rangers then stomped unhindered through the great front court, up the marble steps, and into the baroque halls.

The President, who had lived much of his life in Paris and was a punctilious gentleman of the old international school, ticked off Briceño for his atrocious manners. We may be sure that the Colonel felt a little uncomfortable, but his Ranger training had not been for naught—he soon had the President bundled into an Air Force station wagon which hustled him off to ten days of detention in the captain's cabin of a Navy transport.

This combined-forces operation was a modest model of a coup d'état—swift, cohesive, decisive, yet mutually accommodating and consequently bloodless, even rather tidy. It deposed the President, banned the Parliament, annulled the presidential elections of the preceding month, and established a junta: two Army generals, an admiral, and an Air Force general.

Constitutionalism was overthrown, the military claimed, to preserve democracy. How was that so? The military, legally charged with guarding the purity of the electoral process, had announced that the presidential elections had been fraudulent. This was denied by the civil authorities. The argument might be considered as academic because the elections had also failed to elect any president at all.

Since no candidate had received the constitutional one-third minimum necessary to be elected, the new Congress would have to choose the new president. But the majority of the incoming legislature was APRA (American Popular Revolutionary Alliance), against which the military had a grudge for having murdered a number of officers three decades earlier. And the Congress's choice might well have been the APRA candidate, Haya de la Torre, whom the senior military and most Peruvians of wealth detested as a rabble-rousing revolutionary.

The coup disposed of these upsetting possibilities in the name of delivering democracy from fraud. The junta promised that it would prepare the conditions for clean elections in 1963, upon the conclusion of which it would relinquish its stewardship of the nation to an honestly elected government. A year later, it kept its word.

The Kennedy administration's reaction to this traditional sort of Latin-American performance was spectacular. The White House took off like a rocket within hours after the coup was announced. A statement was issued by the State Department. "We must deplore this military coup d'état . . . and are awaiting more complete reports from our Ambassador. . . . Meanwhile our diplomatic relations with

Peru have been suspended."

Here was none of the Bay of Pigs indecision, of letting matters drift. The reaction was predecided and prearranged: if a coup, retaliate with "suspended" diplomatic relations. Prebriefed before the event, the new diplomacy need not wait for "more complete reports from our Ambassador." It need not be reflective, only reflexive.

Washington's response to the Peruvian coup and junta was not a single mistake; it was a case of multiple fallacies.

The first error was procedural. It was an act of confused, impetuous amateurism to "suspend" relations instantly and dramatically because a foreign government had been overthrown by violence, when our national security was not endangered by the event and when Washington did not have more than preliminary reports on which to make a judgment. In such circumstances, speed is not of the essence. Prudence is. The crisis, requiring hawklike, hard-nosed, eye-ball-to-eye-ball fast decisions, was not an American one. It was a Peruvian one.

The second error was that of naïveté. The New Frontiersmen had taken the Punta del Este documents literally. They apparently thought that when everyone signed up for the Alliance for Progress, all would live up to its commandments. Two days after the coup the White House issued a pained statement revealing that "The President has noted the developments in Peru with great concern."

"It is his belief," the circular went on, that the coup "contravened the common purposes inherent to the Interamerican system and most recently restated in the Charter of Punta del Este. . . ."

In the charter, all had "agreed to work together . . . within a framework of developing democratic institutions." And in the declaration adopted at Punta del Este all had undertaken "to improve and strengthen democratic institutions."

Now it is perfectly true that the Peruvian coup was a piece of backsliding. But this was a *macho*, a very male, failing. It was rather like coveting thy neighbor's wife—or his house or ox. It was wrong, of course, if you insist on being literal, but it was a tradition established with Simon Bolivar, and so regarded as forgivable.

The essential naïveté of the Kennedy administration was one that Wilde would have spotted—that after the wedding at Punta del Este, we would remain our own lovely selves, but that through this union we would wreak on our partners a transformation for the better.

The third fallacy was relating diplomatic recognition to democracy. The well-grounded international practice is that a government may be recognized when it is apparently in effective control of at least most of the country and when it acknowledges the nation's international commitments. Relations may be severed because of an unfriendly or hostile act. Or they may be downgraded by withdrawing the ambassador and leaving a chargé d'affaires as a gesture of displeasure over lesser offenses.

By "suspending" relations with a country on the issue of its internal political philosophy and ethics, the Kennedy administration reverted to Wilson's quixotic policy of using diplomatic recognition as a reward-and-punishment system

43

for teaching Latin-American governments democracy. Wilson withheld recognition in 1913 from General Huerta as president of Mexico because he had seized power through a coup d'état. Secretary of State Bryan outlined the disciplinary treatment this way: "It is the purpose of the United States therefore to discredit and defeat such usurpations whenever they occur. The present policy . . . is to isolate General Huerta entirely; to cut him off from foreign sympathy and aid and from domestic credit, whether moral or material, and to force him out."

This high-minded, schoolmasterish treatment did not work. One thing led to another: inflamed anti-Americanism in Mexico; our naval bombardment of Vera Cruz; the turning against us by the "constitutional" faction of Carranza, which we favored; nevertheless, our recognition of that regime; its inability to govern; Pancho Villa's raid across our border; and finally General Pershing's inconclusive punitive expedition into Mexico.

This messy train of events, proceeding from lofty motives, served only to embitter American-Mexican relations. Wilson's attempt to teach a lesson in democracy was worse than a simple failure; it was downright damaging. The Mexican revolution was bound to work itself out in its own violent way—and it did.

Fortunately in the case of Peru, the Kennedy administration drew back from following through on the Wilsonian curriculum. But its proctoring impulses remained strong. Its only outlet left was rhetoric and stopping aid. The White House and the State Department, therefore, continued their lectures on the necessity of representative and constitutional governments responsive to the "popular will."

Plagued by the realities of a less than perfect world, Washington's performance was not wholly consistent. Following the Peruvian coup, the constitutional government of Guatemala was overthrown. After a minimum of grumbling, the State Department recognized the usurping colonel.

Next was Ecuador. There the "popular will" was represented by a president both constitutionally elected and constitutionally a lush. In disgust and with ease, the military gave the people's intemperate choice the bum's rush. Washington quickly accepted the junta with relief.

But with the coups in the Dominican Republic and Honduras, Washington caused relations to "lapse," recalled ambassadors and cut off aid.

Yet in the case of Yemen, the American government prematurely recognized an insurgent, usurping military regime when it was in shaky control of only a fraction of the country and was violating international obligations to its neighbors.

And in the case of South Vietnam, the military overthrow of a constitutionally elected civilian government, if not encouraged, was at least welcomed by Washington.

The public contradictions and foul-up over recognition were caused by the fitful introduction of democracy as a qualification for recognition. There was really little excuse for such fuzziness. The White House and the State Department would have fared better had they done their homework, absorbed the lessons of Wilson's trying to treat the Mexicans like Princeton undergraduates, and considered the sense of Dean Acheson's calm advice of 1949:

The nature of democracy is such that it can be achieved only from within. . . . Its attainment is essentially a spiritual and personal problem to be solved by the people of each country for themselves. . . .

We maintain diplomatic relations with other countries primarily because we are all on the same planet and must do business with each other. We do not establish an embassy or legation in a foreign country to show approval of its government. We do so to have a channel through which to conduct essential governmental relations and to protect legitimate United States interests. . . .

It is recognition of a set of facts, nothing more. We may have the gravest reservations as to the manner in which it has come to power. We may deplore its attitude toward civil liberties. Yet our long-range objectives in the promotion of democratic institutions may, in fact, be best served by recognizing it and thus maintaining a channel of communication with the country involved.

Military rule in the underdeveloped countries of Asia and Latin America is not a rare, abnormal phenomenon. In Asia, during the years 1953–63, there were at various times governments controlled by military men in Turkey, Syria, Iraq, Pakistan, Burma, Thailand, South Vietnam, and South Korea. In Latin America it was Argentina, Colombia, Cuba, the Dominican Republic, Ecuador, El Salvador, Guatemala, Haiti, Honduras, Nicaragua, Paraguay, Peru, and Venezuela.

This prevalence of military governments has not been simply for lust of power. The reasons are more broadly based.

The American tendency is to look upon rule by soldiers in simplified forms. This view goes a long way back, basically to our own colonial experience with the Red Coats. Our traditional antipathy has been fed and influenced during the first half of this century by our sketchy melodramatic knowledge of Latin-American caudillos and Chinese warlords.

The caudillo was a Latin-American institution during the nineteenth century and first half of the twentieth. He was a general who seized power and ruled arbitrarily until another general, through intrigue and force, threw him out. Late in this era, a vulgarized version of the caudillo appeared, the up-from-the-ranks dictator exemplified by Trujillo and Batista. These were the underworld in epaulets.

The other image of the composite in the American mind was the Chinese warlord. He was a sinister figure: untutored, rapacious, extortionate, and very likely an un-filter-tipped opium smoker. Warlord and caudillo combined, the effect on the American imagination was not reassuring.

But this vision is now somewhat outdated. The modern military dictators favor national planning commissions and some try to rally and manipulate people in the mass, contriving an exclusive political party for this purpose. Often they profess a belief in that elastic thing referred to as "socialism," and may even support Moral Rearmament.

The change in the nature and outlook of military governments has been taking place since the Bolshevik revolution and the occurrence of totalitarianism in Western Europe. Generals as well as politicians became aware of the utility of ideology and the effectiveness of ruling through and in the name of the masses. None, however, used the classic communist stratagem for seizing power. They did not need to, for they themselves usually controlled the principal instruments of coercion—the armed forces.

Modern military dictators might be loosely divided into two groups: the managerial military and the ideological military.

Perhaps the first of the modern military dictators was Mustafa Kemal Ataturk. Although he wrought a political and social revolution in Turkey, he managed the transformation without any pretense that the impulse for it came from the masses. In that sense he did not follow the totalitarian pattern. His was a hero-inspired and directed nationalist revolution. It was also one designed to hoist Turkey once and for all out of medievalism into the twentieth century. In a way it was as drastic a convulsion as the Mexican revolution. But it was under single direction and control; it was not competitively chaotic.

Chiang Kai-shek, following his seizure of power in 1927, also emphasized nationalism and sought to modernize China, but he had been strongly influenced by his Soviet advisers and attempted to adapt some of his lessons in totalitarianism to developing Sun Yat-sen's imprecise Three People's Principles into an ideology and the Kuomintang into a semi-authoritarian party in a one-party state.

In no other great power during the third and fourth decades of this century did the military exert such authority as in Japan. Particularly in the case of the Army, the ideological motivation was intense. But it was peculiarly Japanese in content and idiom: chauvinism blended with a moody, bloodily fatalistic mysticism. Such an ideology was not readily communicable to others—except by samurai sword.

The Army sensed the need of a made-in-Japan export ideology. The Germans and the Italians had put on impressive shows with nazism and fascism. The Russians had used the Communist party effectively as an instrument of control wherever Soviet power was established in Asia. So the Japanese made a try in "Manchukuo." There the Kwantung Army, Japan's elite force on the continent, made its scrofulous Manchurian puppets form a single party with an ersatz totalitarian ideology. Neither took hold.

The Japanese Army officer corps was mostly of peasant or village origin. With reason, it regarded itself as close to and representative of the people. It scorned and envied the *zaibatsu*, the economic power concentrations. But preoccupied with foreign conquest and dependent upon the *zaibatsu* for the material support of its campaigns, the Army was not the domestic revolutionary force that it might otherwise have been.

In Argentina, Peron's military regime was a revolutionary force. It borrowed from fascism its form and its demagogic appeal to the masses. The Peronista combination of personal vanity, social radicalism, and bombastic nationalism pleased the populace, but its wild incompetence and corruption were so damaging to the national economy that, when the regime was overthrown after a decade, Argentina found itself an economic shambles.

Colonel Nasser was confronted in Egypt with far more difficult problems than Colonel Peron: overpopulation, accumulated mass poverty, illiteracy, and limited resources. His Arab socialism assailed the sure-fire demons: the rich and the foreigner. He nationalized economic enterprises, his most flamboyant expropriation being the Suez Canal. This led to war, in which he was saved by John Foster Dulles and Nikita Sergeyevich Khrushchev.

Nasser accepted aid from East and West. Many in the West, underestimating the strength of his nationalism, at first warned that Nasser had aligned himself with the Soviet bloc. To the contrary, Nasser took from the U.S.S.R., gave few favors in return, and occupied himself with his own expansion in Syria, Iraq, and Yemen. At the same time, as head of the senior African republic, he asserted interest in all developments on that continent. And as one of the nonaligned big three, he acted along with Tito and Nehru as spokesman for a composite ethical stance pretending to reflect the conscience of mankind.

The Nasser performance, it must be admitted, had class. Unscrupulous and a little on the flashy side, it still had class. No other of the ideological military fraternity has shown the versatility of Nasser. His greatest skill, perhaps, was in the manipulation of mass media.

To be sure, he has not solved his country's economic problems. Nor is he likely to. But then it is difficult to imagine any feasible alternative doing any better, and easy to envisage others doing worse in a staggering if not impossible situation.

The ideological military shade off into what may be called the managerial military. Field Marshal Ayub Khan, president of Pakistan, is an example. A pukka officer in the Sandhurst tradition, Ayub Khan was not drawn to embrace politically the great unwashed with the ideological affectations of, say, a Peron.

Nor did the field marshal find democracy suitable to Pakistan's needs. "Politicians think that to be respectable a country must retain the exact forms of government obtaining in the United States or Britain," he told Robert Trumbull of the *New York Times* in 1962. "But many new countries will fail if they conform, and in the wake of failure will come chaos and then Communism."

Parliamentary government had not been a success in Pakistan. President Mirza, in 1958, declared martial law, annulled the constitution, dismissed the government, and dissolved the Assembly and all political parties. Mirza resigned and Ayub Khan thereupon took over the government in 1958. However, the compulsions of international respectability, the pressures to pay at least lip service to democracy, caused the field marshal to compromise with his natural inclination to command. He and his collaborators contrived in 1959 a "basic democracy" whereby approximately every one thousand citizens elected one representative. These representatives, called "basic democrats," totaled about eighty thousand, and it was they who elected national and provincial officials.

General Ibrahim Abboud, president of Sudan, was another no-nonsense type. As reported in the press of October 6, 1961, the general observed: "We do not need to import into our country a democracy foreign to our people. . . . Implantation of foreign democratic systems has proved unsuitable to many of the African societies because of the difference in tradition, culture, and social setup."

In Burma, too, the foreign democratic system proved to be unsuitable. It was languid, frivolous, and corrupt. So in 1962, the military, headed by General Ne Win, overthrew the civilian authorities. The public received the coup with relief and satisfaction.

Although Ne Win began as a managerial type, within a year he was on the way to being one of the ideological military. He concocted and applied Burmese socialism, an extensive program of nationalizing the economy. The results have been economic disorder and decline.

The managerial military at times find themselves at odds with popular movements and so in an anti-ideological position. The students of Rangoon University, like students from the secondary schools on up throughout the underdeveloped world, were inclined to be "leftish," many of them Communists. They decided in July, 1962, shortly after Ne Win seized power, to buck the new military government. One thing led to another, ending with some sixteen students and bystanders killed and sixty wounded. The Army wound up the show by demolishing the Student Union with dynamite and closing Rangoon and Mandalay Universities.

It is in matters like shooting students that the ideological military have the advantage over the old-fashioned warlord or caudillo. Even the taciturn managerial military, if they have taken the precaution of proclaiming themselves socialist, have the draw on the intelligentsia. In unexceptionable defense of the people's revolution they can mow down demonstrators as counterrevolutionaries. Not to invoke the name of socialism, however, is to risk being branded a fascist butcher.

With the benevolent neutrality of the Army, Korean students in April, 1960, to their own and everyone else's surprise, overthrew the corrupt government of Syngman Rhee in a spontaneous outburst of violence. There followed a year of political freedom carried to excess. The disorder, corruption, and license got to be too much for at least part of the Army. On May 15, 1961, a group of about forty puritanical officers seized Seoul in a coup d'état.

General Chung Hee Park and his junta, with no pretensions to an ideology, had a revolutionary impact on the Republic of Korea in the first two years of their rule. They were reported to have practically eliminated graft in the government, cracked down on usury, begun a reorganization of the antiquated family system, and placed economic development on a rational basis.

But then a combination of ineptitude, power corrupting those who held it, factionalism, and staggering national problems reduced the Park regime to a sorry unpuritanical spectacle.

While it would be nonsensical to describe these and other military rulers, both the ideological and the managerial, as all out of the same mold, the majority did come from simple circumstances. The modern military dictators are not of aristocratic lineage, the princely generals. Nor are they from families of great wealth. Most have broad, common roots in the villages or urban middle class. They are of the people.

In another respect there is some similarity among these generals. It is in their personal outlook on the society of which they are a part. In most of these countries, the military-academy graduates (and the priests, on another plane) are the only elements of the society indoctrinated in an allegiance to something greater than themselves or their families. The military thus tends to be, more than any other segment of society, emotionally imbued with, although not necessarily more discriminating in identification of, national interests. This naturally inspires in the military an idealized evaluation of its own qualities.

Feeling itself apart from and superior to the civilian elements, the officer caste has a strong group sense. When the modern military acts against a civilian government, it is usually more or less in concert. Rarely now does a single general lead his particular command against or in competition with other generals. If factionalism shows itself, it is after the armed forces have been in power. Then personal or political rivalries may flare into the open.

This happened in Burma and South Korea. In Iraq, after overthrowing the monarchy, the military was involved in one thousand and one nights of intrigue over Nasserite Arab socialism, Baath Arab socialism, and Iraqui nationalism, with coups and countercoups following one another in mystifying succession.

But in most cases military governments are comparatively stable.

One of the common accusations against military rule is that juntas and dictators guard the interests of the so-called oligarchs, that they are reactionary. They are charged with opposition to the progressive elements, who are asserted to be the only hope for the society in transition to modernity.

Such has often been the case in the past, and may be so

in the future. But the trend is in the other direction. The modern military is inclined to be anti rather than pro the old order. The old conservative elements in Egypt, Burma, Korea, and Iraq had no reason to consider Nasser, Ne Win, Park, and Kassim as their defenders. Most of the modern military are reformist, even revolutionary, in their outlook. They are for "progress" and ready to accept and often force change.

Their problem is to know how to progress. As professional military men, they take command of government rarely with experience in the functioning of civilian enterprises, much less with grounding in the complexities of administering a nation. The results are often deplorable. Yet when their records in administration are compared with the accomplishments of civilian regimes in underdeveloped countries, it must be concluded that the generals have not done so badly. Consider what Ayub Khan achieved in Pakistan against what Nehru did for India, or the slow but orderly development under General Stroessner in Paraguay as against the disheveled, aid-dependent performance of Paz Estenssoro in Bolivia.

Related to the belief that military regimes are reactionary was the New Frontier doctrine that they "are the seedbeds from which communism ultimately springs up." This novel dogma assumably grew out of the administration's Cuba trauma. Castro took over so easily from Batista, when that gangster caudillo had through corruption and abuse alienated not only the people but also his armed forces, that Washington universalized the phenomenon as a law of history applicable to all military regimes.

This was an oversimplification that was not even plausible, unless it were assumed that all military rulers antagonize the citizenry, lose the support of their own troops, and allow a subversive force to consolidate and expand a base area from which to mount an attack on the government. This has not been nor is it likely to be the case with most governments by generals.

Some generals, in coming to power or while holding it, have collaborated with Communists. Chiang Kai-shek did so with outstanding success in 1926–27. Kassim in Iraq was less adept. The Peruvian junta, continuing its old blood feud against the APRA, tried to play the Communists off against that political party. The Communists surprised and rewarded the junta with a versatile display of sabotage, strikes, bank robberies, and rudimentary guerrilla operations. Thus persuaded that its hand was being bitten, when gnawed off to the wrist, the junta cracked down on the Communists, but did not seriously attempt to root out the subversion. It was trying to be democratic, observe civil liberties, and win popularity.

The truth of the matter is that military regimes are no more seedbeds of communism than are civilian regimes. Nor do they necessarily tend to tolerate or collaborate with the Communists any more than do governments run by politicians. Indonesia under Sukarno had the largest Communist party in the free world. And Chile under Alessandri, with one of the strongest democratic traditions in South America, was more vulnerable to communist capture from within, through elections, than any of those states on the continent ruled by generals.

Military regimes are not always regarded as peculiarly oppressive by those living under them. Politicians and intellectuals usually disapprove of them, the former because soldiers tend to throw politicians out of jobs, the latter because of political principles. But the majority in underdeveloped countries are inclined to be more objectively cynical. In their experience, little good can be expected from their rulers, of whatever pretensions. And the idea of governments deriving their just powers from the consent of the governed, if these people are acquainted with the concept, seems quite theoretical. It has little or no relation to the past and present realities of their situation.

Hence what would be oppressive to us might seem benevolent to them. A stern military regime that abridged the liberty of the citizenry but provided security for economic development is preferred over a lax civilian government permitting economic or political disorder. When candid and not saying what he thinks a visiting American would like to hear, the average Asian or Latin-American laborer, farmer, or businessman will confide: "We need a strong hand governing us."

His instincts are right, for the process of development through which these people are passing is deeply disruptive. The status quo is disintegrating, and the new society has not yet taken shape. If they are to have any chance of making the grade, the government must maintain order.

The basic issue is not whether the government is dictatorial or is representative and constitutional. The issue is whether the government, whatever its character, can hold the society together sufficiently to make the transition. It is not how the ruling authority came to power but whether it effectively and constructively disposes of its power.

The natural progression of the developmental process is, first, the maintenance of order, of a fundamental discipline in the society. Then it is economic growth. It is creating wealth to make a middle class with a vested interest in stability and to pay for the public facilities, particularly education, that are essential preconditions to democracy. Finally, as a product of this slow, organic growth, reliably representative government and constitutionalism may come to flourish.

In placing first emphasis on democracy, the New Frontiersmen neglected what they had learned from Hamilton, Madison, and Jay. Times have not changed that much. It is still true that constitutionalism and democracy, as well as economic growth, cannot develop and be preserved except on a foundation of order and stability.

Order and stability are maintained either voluntarily or by coercion. They are maintained voluntarily when there is a broad consensus in the society and an accepted tradition of tolerant self-control, accepting the will of the majority. As such conditions rarely exist in underdeveloped societies that have broken with the old dispensation and are in transition, order and stability, if attainable, are achieved through coercion.

This does not necessarily mean constant harsh repression. It means that the government restrains the excessive demands of a population that wants the benefits of a developed society before it has earned them. It also means that the government will crush subversion against itself with such force as is necessary.

A civilian government may force through development if the leadership is strong, intelligent, and decisive and has the support of its armed forces and police. As a Venezuelan official put it in simplified form to Richard Eder of *The New York Times:* "It is not enough to be a good man. You must be firm and clever, too."

The Venezuelan was speaking of Juan Bosch, evicted in 1963 from the presidency of the Dominican Republic by the military. "Bosch may have been a good man, but he was neither firm nor clever. His conscience may be at rest, but so is he—in exile."

Now Bosch had been a favorite of Washington because he was of the noncommunist left, just the ticket to save Latin America from Castroism and for democracy. The hitch was that the noncommunist-left formula, workable in most of the mature and stable countries of Western Europe, was not generally applicable to turbulent Latin America—or Asia or Africa.

To be sure, Betancourt had gotten away with it in Venezuela because he was barely firm and quite clever enough. Also, Venezuela had a large, assured income from oil and iron exports. And Betancourt was lucky. But this one non-communist-leftist swallow did not make a democratic summer for Latin America.

The nature of most civilian leaders, liberal and conservative, is that they want to be popular. Their inclination is toward going along with the wishes of the people which, in underdeveloped countries, are often conflicting and usually ignorant, extravagant, and unattainable. So like surfboard riders, the leaders try to balance themselves atop a breaking comber, more or less cleverly adjusting themselves to the agitation below while praying that they may last out the ride. The performance can be, as was President Goulart's in Brazil and Sukarno's in Indonesia, breathtaking for the spectator. But is it government?

The combination of exaggerated public expectations and the leaders' desire for popularity tends to make politicians into demagogues. And demagogues must have devils to exorcize from the body politic. The conventional devils are the "reactionary" rich and foreigners. But in attacking these two, the masses and their demagogues drive out what they need for economic growth—domestic and foreign private investment.

Now to restrain popular unrest, to hold it in line with the pace of economic development, may in many cases be beyond the ability of any government, civilian or military. Where this is so, the regime is in serious trouble, for there is no law that says an underdeveloped country can go in only one direction—progressively forward.

The primary need of stability, order, and coercion might suggest that military rule is more suitable than civilian government for many underdeveloped countries. The military may be more effective than its civilian alternative only if it is better able—as it has not always been—to exercise control. And the generals would have to be not only firm but also clever, which they have not always been, largely because of ignorance of how the life of a nation functions and, more importantly, grows.

Whether suitable or not, military regimes are likely to

increase in number. The trend in the underdeveloped part of the world is not toward democracy but toward authoritarianism. As many civilian governments fail to cope with the huge dilemmas of development, as demagogy plunges toward chaos, the primitive reaction is for the military, sooner or later, to take over government.

The American people will not approve of this. But it is a fact of life on this globe. And they will have to learn to live with it because they will not be able to change it.

Imbalance of Terror

*T*here is a certain scientific symmetry between war by atoms and war by asteroids. To achieve the requisite nuclear explosive force, science exploited the universe of that which is too small to be seen by the naked eye. In speculating about bombing a selected section of the world with an asteroid pilfered from outer space, science ventures out to that part of the universe too far to be seen by the naked eye.

The theory of assault by heavenly body is less interesting for its scientific ingenuity than for the example it provides of the lengths to which the human mind can go in quest of weapons of mass destruction.

The theory, as reported in the press of January 19, 1962, was presented before the American Astronautical Society and envisaged the possible use of a superrocket to chivvy an asteroid out of accustomed orbit into collision with the earth, with perhaps an 80 million megaton yield. It was anticipated, according to the news report, that both the United States and the Soviet Union would have rockets and crews capable of such missions by about 1970. A single sortie asteroid strike pinpointing on, say, Kentucky would dispose of, it was predicted, the area from Boston to Miami, Duluth to New Orleans, and Washington, D.C., to Omaha, with probable resultant earthquakes toppling all remaining buildings in North America.

A near miss, bursting in the Atlantic, the account continued, would produce tidal waves probably destroying the eastern seaboard of the United States and much of Western Europe. Finally it is to be noted that an ample stockpile of asteroid weapons already exists, assumably thousands of these counterforce, preemptive weapons, invulnerably dispersed between Mars and Jupiter, awaiting a nudge in the desired direction.

This ultimate in man's arrogance may never come to pass. The infinite neutrality of the firmament toward human hates and fears may be violated, to be sure, in other ways, most obviously from man-made satellites. It would seem superfluous, however, to the ends sought to make ballistic use of celestial spheres when the weapons handily available on earth have the capability of so generous an overkill.

No one is really happy about this condition of abundance. And the continuing growth and diversification of nuclear, chemical, biological, and bacteriological weapons is detranquilizing. There are, of course, probably hundreds of millions in Africa, Asia, and Latin America who are only dimly aware or even ignorant of what these extensive and complex systems of warfare signify. But most people have a rough idea of the implications of modern arms, if only of the nuclear spectaculars.

The consequent sense of collective insecurity expresses itself futilely at one extreme in ban-the-bomb protests. At the other it is manifested in the fatalism usually accorded to lightning on a lake—since there is nothing that you or I can do to prevent a sudden storm, why forgo the pleasures of boating?

The nuclear missile weapons, dominating the military scene and the public imagination, have been for attack, for the offensive. We are at the stage, not unfamiliar in history, when a new weapon has revolutionized the ratio of strength between the offense and the defense. It has been said that with the conventional weapons of World War II, the defense had a three to one advantage over the offense. With the nuclear missile, the advantage passed overwhelmingly to the offense and by the early 1960's was practically total.

No effective defensive weapons system had been developed, although we, the British, and the Russians had been striving to devise counterarms. The only defense against nuclear missile attack was the threat of a counteroffensive in kind.

As we and the Russians raced to increase and perfect our offensive weapons system, while desperately seeking the defensive answers to one another's inventiveness, we each had three basic choices of strategy. One was the strategy of counterforce. A second was the finite deterrent concept. Finally, as an extension of the second, there was the graduated deterrent.

Counterforce is essentially an offensive concept. In simplified terms, it envisages an assault on the enemy's nuclear capabilities, rather than on his cities, and battening down one's own population in shelters to lessen the manpower loss from a retaliatory strike by any surviving part of the victim's strategic forces. Thus the war could be, it is hoped, continued and won.

The theory is couched of course in terms of defense: counterforce would be loosed in response to a *casus belli*. It is held that the threat of counterforce attack is sufficient to deter both a nuclear attack and lesser aggressions. Conventional forces might be, therefore, practically superfluous because the injured party would proceed directly from protests and warnings to massive retaliation. In this strategy there is a particularly high premium on being the first to strike.

For us, counterforce was a plausible concept during the 1950's when we had overwhelming nuclear superiority and when delivery was by aircraft. Delivery by bombers from airfields meant approximately the same to the United States and the Soviet Union: an operable margin of warning, a fighting chance of interception, and big bases that were relatively vulnerable launching sites for nuclear attack. If the aggressor could accept severe attrition from interceptors and had enough to keep coming, he might succeed in demolishing the nests of nuclear retaliation and so "win." It was our superiority over the Russians in this respect that made counterforce a tenable American doctrine in the fifties.

Had our government wholeheartedly and systematically adopted the counterforce strategy, we would have begun intensive nationwide preparation of shelters to limit population loss from the enemy's second strike following our massive retaliation, or from the Soviet Union's beating us to the draw with a preemptive strike. We made no such preparations. And had we begun such a program, the

U.S.S.R. would have had reason to believe that we were readying ourselves for attack and might have been tempted to try to forestall it by striking before our shelter preparations were well advanced.

By the early 1960's missile delivery of nuclear warheads was becoming operational. Warning of transpolar attack shrank to about fifteen minutes. Missile launching positions were being made less vulnerable, either through going statically underground or mobilely underseas. Still no dependable defense against missile attack had been developed. Either side could penetrate the other's interception.

But having done that, what then? The critical targets were no longer sprawling airfields and exposed bombers. They were dispersed missiles in hardened, deep silos, destroyable only with extraordinary precision or by salvos, or they were in submarines moving about underwater and under arctic ice. Failure of an attempt to demolish these retaliatory capabilities would ensure a counter onslaught on easily demolished cities. One could still preempt the initiative, but it became increasingly doubtful that one could preempt victory.

American and Soviet cities remained open, their populations uncovered. Nor did people move away from these attractive targets. The American public barely took notice in the press of May, 1962, of the reported estimate of Mr. Stewart L. Pittman, Assistant Secretary of Defense for Civil Defense, that in the event of a massive nuclear strike on the United States in the late 1960's or early 1970's, about a hundred and ten million Americans would be killed. A marginal forty to fifty-five million would die or survive, depending upon whether they had shelters. Some thirty-five million, out of range, might, it was said, survive without protection.

Each side had the other's population as hostages, while lavishing protection on its growing family of arms. And as the possibilities of fireball surprise approached the instantaneous, the likelihood of terrible retribution approached the inevitable. The need for finger-on-the-button alert lessened.

So everyone settled down into a more or less accepted balance of terror that was only occasionally terrifying. This was the essence of the finite deterrent.

The very nomenclature, balance of terror and finite deterrent, indicated that this was not a "win" policy. It was suited to the realities of the situation, a recognition that there could probably be no nuclear win. Under the circumstances, victory would have to be sought through means other than nuclear interchange—hence Mr. Khrushchev's dogma of coexistence, the unconventional hostilities in Southeast Asia with conventional weapons, and our own frantic efforts to attract the "uncommitted" and hold the "committed" by aid and homilies.

Balance of terror, however, can be counted on only as it produces a nuclear and emotional equilibrium. To achieve this requires an unorthodox approach. Each side would have to accept the desirability of overkill plenitude for the other to avoid anxieties over megaton inadequacy and consequent impulsive nuclear behavior. Big, dirty warheads should probably be welcomed as manifestations of defensive intent. A systematic attempt to shelter people would be suspiciously provocative. Self-limitations on invulnerable deterrents would in some cases be prudent—our 1963 budget set a finite plateau of forty-one Polaris submarines, beyond which number, it has been suggested, these missile carriers could come to be viewed no longer as charged with obliterating cities but as having a sinister salvo mission against Soviet nuclear capabilities.

Balance of terror, then, can attain equilibrium only if both sides are rational and engage in tacit cooperation to maintain stability in the balance—more particularly, to avoid failure of communication, misunderstanding, accidents, and sudden panic. During the early sixtys both governments appeared to have behaved rationally with regard to nuclear weapons. There has been little evidence of tacit understanding.

There are three reasons why we cannot rely on the concept of the balance of terror. While we may assume continuing White House and Joint Chiefs of Staff rationality, we cannot be sure that the Kremlin and the Soviet high command will always behave rationally. Nor can we count on the Kremlin to cooperate, even tacitly, to maintain a steady equilibrium in a balance of terror. Finally, a technological breakthrough by one side with a new defensive system would upset the balance. So might the development of an offensive weapons system decisively superior to nuclear missiles—for example, beam-directed energy weapons operating from space.

During its first year in office, the Kennedy administration, acting on an erroneous assumption that the United States suffered from a missile gap, apparently decided to maintain an arms and target mix—something of everything

—and what may be described as a strategy of graduated deterrent. While holding invulnerable deterrents in reserve, implicitly threatening the decimation of Soviet "control centers" (meaning cities), we would resist conventional challenges with conventional weapons. For this we needed a potent conventional force. If the challenge were pressed beyond our capacity to resist with these means, we would escalate our response into local use of tactical nuclear weapons.

After discovering that the missile gap was in our favor and after a buildup of American nuclear power was under way, Secretary of Defense McNamara proposed in June, 1962, that in a nuclear war the principal military objectives should be "the destruction of the enemy's military forces, not of his civilian population," meanwhile holding "sufficient reserve striking power to destroy an enemy society if driven to it." Mr. Khrushchev's response to this proposal for another rung in escalation—a try at pre-emption before mass retaliation—was pious outrage and a statement that "nuclear missile war entirely erases the line between the battlefield and the rear. It is the civilian population that will be the first prey of the weapons of mass annihilation."

This oblique dialogue seems to have left matters pretty much as they had been—obscure and unpredictable. There is, however, one thing that we and the Soviet Union can share in common: anxiety over the Nth-country problem. This is the proliferation of nuclear capabilities among many states.

British possession of nuclear arms has been a source of assurance, not concern, to us. The French potential has been worrisome because of its independence of NATO and the uncertainties over future French policies. The serious misgivings relate to, particularly, Red China and the ten to fifteen other nations that by 1970 are expected to have acquired nuclear arms. The possibilities for atomic mischief-making are impressive.

The classic example of this is the Nth-state-rogue submarine lobbing a nuclear missile onto an American or Soviet city, thereby perhaps setting off an unwanted exchange between the nuclear giants. It has been suggested that the only protection against such provocation would be the withdrawal of all American and Soviet missile submarines from the high seas.

Another troublesome possibility would be overt action by a minor ally against the other side, embroiling the major ally, with the hostilities then spiraling into full nuclear war. Should Moscow and Peking reconcile their differences, Chinese fanaticism, implicating the U.S.S.R., would pose this tricky prospect. Our hope in such a situation would be that the Russians, for sufficient reasons of their own, would decline to be involved and that the matter would be left between us and the Chinese.

Membership in the nuclear club will continue to grow after 1970 as the initiation requirements become less costly and easier. And for those who would not wait, there are the economy-package do-it-yourself weapons of mass destruction. These are the simpler systems of chemical, biological, and bacteriological warfare.

The proliferation in kinds of weapons was contemporaneous with the proliferation of states. From the fragmentation of the old empires appeared the new sovereignties, each with its peculiar hopes, hurts, hates, and pretensions. Many of these states had governments which could scarcely be described as either stable or responsible. The combination of proliferating arms and proliferating irresponsibility does not brighten the distant prospect.

Perhaps there is no solution to the widening gap between man's overdeveloped weapon cunning and his underdeveloped social wisdom. Perhaps man is condemned to extinction by his own folly, fear, pride, and wile. But before we so conclude, we should look at what are recommended to us as the possible routes to salvation from disintegration.

The theories for creating order out of the world's anarchy in armaments derive from varying estimates of human nature. One view holds that man, if not a predatory animal, is certainly a combative one and that those peoples who have been domesticated to the degree that they lost their pugnacity have always gone down before the barbarians, the killers, the authentic man.

Therefore, if man is to be saved from his own indiscriminate belligerency, with weapons that now threaten to cause, when not his decimation, his deformation in the womb, the solution must be imposed by force—implicitly and, if necessary, explicitly applied. Talk of self-restraint, negotiated disarmament, multilateral treaties, and universal rule of law is twaddle. Peace will come only out of selective violence, order out of a passage through localized disorder, security out of peril.

Proceeding from this view, the theory logically evolves to a belief that the general anarchy in armaments will be resolved only if one state—and it must be a powerful one to do the job—unilaterally imposes and maintains control over the world's arms. The choice, then, would be between a Pax Americana and a Pax Sovietica.

The concept of this country's imposing a Pax Americana has two present defects. One is that the favorable opportunity has passed, at least for the time being. A showdown with the Soviet Union might have been successful during the period from the end of World War II to the end of the Korean War when we had at first an atomic monopoly and then a definite nuclear superiority, without the possibility of heavy nuclear retaliation. During this span we had the punitive wherewithal to back up a demand for Soviet nuclear sterilization.

Our ultimatum that the Kremlin abandon nuclear arms development and accept inspection could have been supported by graduated threats of punishment, and fulfillment thereof, up to and including what is called preventive war. However, the Russians who, with all their realism, are hypersensitive on matters of sovereignty would probably not have yielded and we would have ended up in a general war with objectives limited at the outset to denying the U.S.S.R. nuclear capabilities but soon vaguely extending. We probably would have destroyed Soviet nuclear capability but at heavy cost, very likely including Soviet occupation of Western Europe.

While the optimum time for such a showdown has passed, a new opportunity may occur if we make a breakthrough with an effective defense system against missiles, or new offensive weapons outmoding nuclear missiles, and the Soviet

Union does not. If the Russians make a breakthrough before we do, the opportunity will be theirs.

The situation is now complicated by other nations' having nuclear arms. While the Kremlin would not scruple at trying to impose by force its unitary control over the world's arms, it is implausible to suppose that we might attempt to disarm also such countries as Britain and France.

Therein lies the second defect of the Pax Americana theory. We are really not people of that kidney. To set about denying nuclear arms to the U.S.S.R. and others by a systematic, self-disciplined exercise in mounting coercion, culminating probably in nuclear war—that is not in our makeup. Scarcely more credible would be the idea of our being willing and even able to police indefinitely the unthankful survivors.

No nation is quicker to remorse and self-reproach, none more pining to be loved by foreigners, few less possessed by convictions of mission. The Pax Americana theory is as alien to our nature as a Pax Sovietica is natural to the Leninist outlook.

Another theory for bringing the anarchy in armaments under control stems from a depreciation of such elemental forces as power rivalries, antagonistic beliefs, racial hatreds, and neurotic national anxieties. This theory is preoccupied with the contrivance of legal restraints on weapons and fighting men. The attention is focused on the instrumentalities, not the causes—which are unmanageable by disarmament conferences.

Past efforts at arms control and disarmament give scant hope for future attempts. If arms control or disarmament agreements are reached, they will have been preceded by a radical improvement in the international situation and will be little more than a confirmation of basic realities.

The U.S.S.R. and even more Red China at their present fanatic and therefore immature stage of social evolution oppose our conception of a world of live and let live. They have no wish to reduce tensions which they can manipulate. They exist on a synthetic dynamism, now that the spontaneous fires of revolution are burned down. Their dynamism pulses between calculated positive and negative charges— in the field of war, between appeals for absolute, unattainable disarmament, which they would not themselves accept, and war scares from the fulfillment of which the Soviet Union has thus far backed away. If this dynamism, internally and externally, is allowed to subside, the society loses its revolutionary character and the professional revolutionaries who are its rulers risk losing power.

A related theory, also relying on form rather than underlying substance, envisages increasing United Nations authority and the reduction of national sovereignties to the extent that states abandon or drastically cut their warmaking capacity and come to rely on a UN peace force for international security and order. Few governments trust the UN enough to dispose of their defenses in such a fashion. And the communist states would either sanctimoniously sabotage the realization of this "bourgeois" dream or flatly turn it down.

Nor is it conceivable that the American people would accede to a UN peace force with such power that the United States would be physically unable to resist it, and so subject themselves to a motley supergovernment. Such a dispensation, in the remote event that it were achieved, would almost certainly be either ineffectual or pernicious.

With a Pax Americana not feasible, armament control a present and foreseeable fantasy, and a polyglot posse an unacceptable proposition, what is left? There is the possibility of an imposed Pax Sovietica if the Soviet Union alone gains a decisive weapon advantage that effectively protects both its striking force and its population. We can hardly regard this as a solution, only as a catastrophe. But it could happen, to which our best and necessary response is to get such a system before the Russians do.

There remains a hope, with no pretensions to surety. If the peoples of the world can sweat out the next decade or two, provided that this time of grace is granted, several developments may occur to temper man's preposterous power of negation. These developments have to do with what people think and feel, not with universalized pacts.

We can hope that as the overkill capacity swells, the grisly absurdity of nuclear war repopularizes conventional weapons as the instruments for prosecuting national conflicts by war. Because these conflicts will persist, the hope in dealing with the inevitable is that everyone remembers that wars, after all, are fought for finite gains at finite costs.

Such an unspoken understanding is not without precedent. Chemical warfare, used in World War I, was avoided in World War II. One can hope that resort to chemical, biological, bacteriological, and nuclear weapons will be likewise inhibited in future wars.

More basic, however, is the issue of fanaticism, most dangerously the Communists' apocalyptic view of their role in human history and, hence, their compulsions to dynamism. Fanaticism has in the past raged and then faded as it was forced to come to terms with reality. The same will happen with communism. The question is how long this will take. There is no fixed span for the exhaustion of fanaticism.

Our hope must be an affirmative one—that we, the Western Europeans, the Japanese, Canadians, Australians, and New Zealanders, continue to outperform the Russians, Chinese, and other extremists. If we can demonstrate an increasing superiority not only in military and economic matters but also in civilized character, we shall find an invigorating fulfillment of ourselves and in the process will have done more than we otherwise could to frustrate and disabuse fanaticism.

This process may goad the communist rulers to desperate action. Or confronted with impressive reality they may gradually feel compelled to seek accommodation to a vital, moderate, and versatile West. This is our affirmative course. There is no other.

Paul Bunyan and
the United Nations

*O*f itself, the United Nations is not important. But for the United States, it is important.

It is important as a psychological problem within ourselves. It is a psychological problem because there is a conflict between our wishes about the UN and the reality of the UN. Although the conflict is subsiding, into disillusion or cynicism, it still troubles many. For the origins of our wishes go deep in our nature.

Morality and idealism are insistent strains in the American tradition. As the UN was brought into existence after World War II, these qualities were invoked for it and responded to. The UN was moral because it was against war and for peace and human harmony. It was idealistic because its charter set forth these moral commitments as goals to be attained. Represented as an absolute good, it was a cause appealing for allegiance.

The American attachment to the UN was also more subtly involved. Many Americans felt that the United States should right a wrong preying on its conscience—our rejection of membership in the League of Nations. Had the United States been a part of the League, they thought, somehow World War II might have been avoided. This fault would be compensated for by support of the UN. Furthermore, we felt compelled to do everything possible so that our conscience could never in the future be troubled by similar self-reproach.

Through our atomic monopoly, we had attained world supremacy from which we shrank, for we have always felt that there was something immoral about power and the necessities that attend its possession. We sensed that the UN might be a way to evade that disreputable side effect of accession to paramount strength in the world.

Instinctively we were impelled toward the UN. There, we hoped, we could share our power with others and avoid apparent responsibility for its iniquitous possession. We would turn our backs on isolation and become internationalist, without imperialist taint, innocent in our might.

In one light these were gentle, generous instincts. In another light they could be regarded as power prudery, for our attitudes with regard to power have always had a touch of sanctimony, accompanied by the prude's occasional lapses from grace—the long misuse of power in our policy of apartheid toward the American Indian and our aggressive spree in the war against Spain.

Whether noble or prudish, our instincts about power and the UN were, in any case, illusions. Power could not be shared in the fashion that we wistfully fancied.

We had a feeling of desperation about the UN that heightened the conflict between our wishes and the eternal realities. The world organization, we believed, was mankind's last hope. Without it, national rivalries and conflicts would lead to wars with the new weapons—and desolation. The UN, therefore, must be made to work. It had to work. Otherwise all hope would be lost.

Yet we have come to suspect that the UN may fail, or even that it has already failed. We know that as a moral force in the world its voice is weak and incoherent. We know that it does not presently dispose of significant authority. We have seen states as diverse as the U.S.S.R., France, India, and Cuba ignore or rebuff the UN when they felt that it was intrusive in what they claimed were their internal affairs. And it is plain to all that the organization is close to bankruptcy.

Still we applaud the declamations of our own and of foreign statesmen proclaiming that the UN is the only alternative to war while quietly doubting that this is so. We admire the influential, decent, and vocal segment of world opinion which pays total tribute to the UN while wishing that we could believe what they are saying and wondering if they themselves do.

Having sponsored the UN's creation and having lavished affection, care, and keep on it, we shrink from seeing it as a great world power must see it. Anxious to preserve and invigorate it, we ask too much of it and charge it with responsibilities it cannot support. Because our ambitions for the UN exceed its abilities, we jeopardize the lesser constructive contribution to peace on earth that it could make.

The exaggerated expectations regarding the UN began

with the writing of the charter. The exhausted victors of World War II, speaking as "We the people of the United Nations," expressed their determination, among other things, to save succeeding generations from the scourge of war, to reaffirm their faith in fundamental human rights, to establish conditions under which justice could be maintained, and for these ends to practice tolerance and unite their strength to maintain international peace and security.

The purposes of the UN were declared to be, it is sufficient to say, to develop friendly relations among nations, to achieve international cooperation, and to be a center for harmonizing the actions of nations. Membership was to be open to all peace-loving states. Sovereign equality of all of its members was a basic principle.

The turning over of a new leaf to inscribe a charter, solemnly adhered to, could not alter the intemperate forces at work in the world. The American and Western European values embodied in the UN and the Western parliamentary form in which the organization was cast, while familiar to the communist and underdeveloped governments, were not always congenial to them and were readily susceptible to their conscious or subconscious sabotage.

In its first line, the charter soared rhetorically above reality: "We the peoples of the United Nations. . . ."

In truth, governments and not peoples were the makers and executors of the charter. In the case of the United States, the other Western democracies, and a few others, it was credible to assume that those who signed the charter did, indeed, in the final analysis sign on behalf of the peoples for whom they spoke. But in the case of the representatives of the U.S.S.R., Byelorussia, Cuba, the Dominican Republic, Egypt, Iran, Poland, the Ukraine, Saudi Arabia, Yugoslavia, and so on, for whom did the delegates of these governments speak?

To go to the source, a rather old-fashioned one and hence readily intelligible, had such a question been asked of Abdul Aziz Ibn Abdur Rahman al Faisal al Saud, then king of Saudi Arabia, he would have answered that his delegates spoke for him, naturally, and he for "we, the Saudi Arabian people"—for who else would and who but Allah could dare to contest his legitimacy for doing so? To which there could have been no counter.

Nor could there have been one to a similar response from Stalin or Trujillo, for an organization that pretends to near universality cannot inquire sharply into matters of legitimacy and who represents whom.

The attribute of "peace-loving," like other forms of loving, is subjective and variable. We ourselves had and have a pretty generally agreed idea of what we mean by "peace-loving" state, human rights, justice, tolerance, friendly relations, and international cooperation. The mature democracies of Western Europe, whence most of these principles originated, interpret the rules of the club in a sense similar to ours.

But for the Asian and African anticolonial revolutionaries, the Arab nationalists, and most of all the Marxist-Leninists, the UN precepts are subject to interpretations divergent from ours. Indian peace-loving, for example, was sadistic toward Goa and for some years masochistic with regard to Red China.

The most convenient illustration of this variance, to the point of conflict with us, comes from the Communists. They proclaim themselves to be peace-loving, but their determination, in the words of the charter, "to establish conditions under which justice . . . can be maintained . . ." overrides their attachment to peace to the extent that they advocate, and prosecute, "just" wars. Concretely, the communist military operations in Laos and South Vietnam were "just" because armed violence was used to bring about "liberation." In this case liberation meant freeing the Laotians and Vietnamese from the manifold benefits bestowed on them by the United States and, completing the evil chain of sophistry, imposing upon them the degrading system and abject conditions that exist in North Vietnam.

This sophistry and the semantic differences between us and the Communists derive from no simple divergence of opinion between us. They are but superficial manifestations of a belief and doctrine of action not just different from but militantly opposed to ours.

Knowing this, it can hardly be expected that the UN, because it is the UN, can somehow harmonize enmity. Insofar as the UN is an independent personality and not a miscellany of national representatives, it is schizophrenic. Conflicts with the Soviet Empire, which seem insoluble elsewhere, are no more likely to be resolved in the UN. There is no magic in venue. Especially is this so when the institutionalized meeting place is itself regarded as something to be destroyed once its usefulness to the communist conspiracy has passed. For the Communists, the UN is bourgeois in concept and bourgeois in its parliamentary form.

Paul Bunyan and the United Nations

Certain theses adopted at the Second Congress of the Comintern in 1920 were applicable to the UN in 1945 and still are so:

> Communism rejects parliamentarianism as the form of the future. . . . Therefore, there can be a question only of utilizing bourgeois State institutions with the object of destroying them. . . . The Communist Party enters such institutions not in order to do constructive work, but in order to direct the masses to destroy from within the whole bourgeois State machine and Parliament itself.

The folklore that somehow small nations are more decent and dispassionate than big ones, plus the belief in the universal applicability of democratic forms, resulted in a world organization based on the principle of the sovereign equality of all its members. On this principle of all states being equal, the UN defies the law of gravity governing power realities and orbits in a state of political weightlessness, inducing the varying subjective effects noted by spacemen: disequilibrium, nausea (Cosmonaut Titov), euphoria (Astronaut Glenn), and hallucinations (Astronaut Cooper).

It is not that Upper Volta is an unworthy nation undeserving of respect and esteem. It is only that parity among UV, UK, US, and USSR in a world assembly would seem to relate only to the Roman alphabet and their equal vote.

With every state in the UN possessing one vote, there exist strong compulsions, internal and external, for each delegate to raise his hand and be counted on each and every issue even when of remote concern and acquaintance. And so it is not surprising to read that Jaja Wachuku of Nigeria recommended to the General Assembly in 1961 as a solution to the great-power deadlock the surrender of Berlin to the UN and the assignment of the UN force in the Congo, when withdrawn from that duty, to policing Berlin, with control turned over to the smaller nations.

Mr. Wachuku was not alone in his exhilaration with global issues, temptingly distant from the nagging, baffling problems of the homeland. Many of the new statesmen frequenting the UN, prominent among whom were Alex Quaison Sackey, Raul Roa, Sukardjo Wirjopranoto, Dondogyo Tsevegmid, and Vengalil Krishan Krishna Menon, were enthusiastic practitioners of busybody diplomacy.

Rarely, one of the new voices speaks in other tones, as did President Senghor of Senegal on October 31, 1961, to the General Assembly:

> We have denounced the imperialism of the great powers only to secrete a miniature imperialism toward our neighbors in the non-aligned group. We have demanded disarmament from the great powers only to transform our countries into arsenals. We proclaim our neutralism but we do not always base it upon a policy of neutrality.

The charter's precept "to practice tolerance and live together in peace with one another as good neighbors" has today a wistful irrelevance. The UN does serve as a forum "to develop friendly relations among nations." But it is also an arena of conspiracy, petty intrigue, and bombast. Some conflicts of national interest may be resolved in the UN, but many are inflamed and spread from local or regional disputes to worldwide proportions.

Paul Bunyan and the United Nations

Were there no UN, leaders who might otherwise be sitting under a thatch roof quietly enjoying the first monsoon rains and perhaps doing a little constructive thinking about raising national productivity find themselves instead in an overheated air-conditioned hassle on Manhattan Island between the Italians and Austrians over an Alpine ethnic minority. Other leaders, did this Parliament of Man not exist might be laying plans for irrigating a stretch of the African desert, but now are themselves irrigated with double-Scotches-on-the-rocks, while soaking up schemes for condemning American imperialist designs against Cuba or for denouncing the perpetuation of British colonialism in the South Arabian Federation.

The level of irresponsibility in the UN will continue to rise with Dr. Jagan's Guiana, Red China, and more freshly cut-adrift colonies in prospect for membership. The sheikdom of Kuwait has become a member of the UN. If Kuwait, why not Sharja and the other Beau Geste sheikdoms of Trucial Oman, beside which Monaco, Andorra, and Lichtenstein tower as models of statehood? The more, perhaps, the merrier, but not, perforce, the wiser.

It is sometimes contended that the UN plays an indispensable role as a seminary in which immature nations can be tutored to stay out of mischief and fit themselves for our kind of international society. This view glosses over the competitive tutelage by the Communists, the presence of mature delinquents in the UN, and the depth of antipathy to our kind of society in the immature nature. In any event the artificial environment of the UN is a poor cram course for international realities.

Missionary schooling of the new statesmen would better be attempted, on our part, through the Department of State in its contacts with embassies in Washington—even if this means the creation of yet another Assistant, Deputy, Under or even Alter Secretary of State—and through our own Foreign Service establishments abroad, where quiet enlightenment of emerging governments is presumably essayed as a customary practice of diplomacy.

The UN has undertaken at various times peace-keeping operations with varying results. Certainly the UN served as a useful tranquilizer in Palestine after Israel had achieved its main objectives, a sedation that could have been administered probably as effectively through the traditional good offices provided by neutrals. But it was an accomplishment, even if an international garrison of five thousand men sweated in the desert at considerable expense until the budget pains of the UN revealed costs of some seventeen million dollars a year for their upkeep.

As for Korea, the weight of the operation was borne by the United States and the South Koreans. The utility of the UN sponsorship was "mobilization" of world opinion, except communist, on our side. It is questionable how much this rallying of favor affected events during and subsequent to the conflict.

The Congo extravaganza was something else. Proceeding from the inherent implausibility of the Congo's emerging as a state in any sense of the word—modern, medieval, or ancient—and its immediate reversion to some of the less winsome mores of primitive folk, we come to the healing ministrations of the UN. These were designed to calm down the excitement, keep the cold war off the equator, and get the Congo on the road to responsible nationhood and into the UN as a peace-loving state. The Congo has been made a vote-casting member of the UN, but there remains something yet to be accomplished on the other counts.

Was the UN the only answer for the essentially impossible, inevitably bloody Congo situation? The alternatives, including resumption of Belgian authority until a more or less orderly transfer of sovereignty could be made, would all have involved fighting. But it is difficult to conjure up a train of events less in harmony with the UN Charter and less desirable as a precedent than that which has occurred since the world organization became seized of the problem.

As for New Guinea, this was one of those shabby international deals that sometimes seem necessary and for which the participants, for mutually contradictory reasons, bestow merit and applause upon themselves.

Indonesia claimed Netherlands New Guinea even though the primitive Papuan natives of New Guinea are of totally different race, culture, and language from the Indonesians. The Dutch proposed that the Papuans be allowed self-determination. This, Indonesia charged, was an attempt "to confuse the national struggle for independence."

In 1962 Sukarno dispatched surface and parachute units to infiltrate Netherlands New Guinea, breathing fire about lining up with the Russians to liberate the simple Papuans. Alarmed by the prospect of a Dutch-American versus Soviet-Indonesian confrontation on this segment of the equator (quite as awkward strategically for the U.S.S.R. as the Congo), Washington moved quickly with dubious good offices to sweep the Dutch and the Papuans under the UN carpet.

Because the Communist and most of the underdeveloped countries accepted Krishna Menon's dogma that colonialism "is a permanent aggression," Washington's tidying up was adopted by the General Assembly. One of the few objectors was little Dahomey which expressed the straitlaced opinion that approval should not be given to the transfer of a population from one nation to another under the threat of war and without provisions for a referendum by the people being trafficked.

Washington, however, preened itself on its peace-keeping diplomacy. And U Thant intoned that this was an "epoch-making precedent" and that it "may well be a step in the gradual evolution of the United Nations as an increasingly effective instrument for the peaceful resolution of differences."

The precedent was, however, something short of epoch-making, for within the same epoch, that is to say within a matter of months, Washington produced another pile of debris from American mediating efforts, also to be swept under the UN carpet. This time it was Yemen with its madly raveled revolution, a Marxist-Nasserite-Thuggee junta against a tribal theocracy with Egyptian, Saudi Arabian, American, British, and Soviet involvements.

Covering up Washington's failure, the UN was to help disentangle Nasser from the land once ruled by the Queen of Sheba. Poor U Thant, an easygoing Burmese Buddhist buffeted by a variety of complicating pressures, obligingly sent General Carl von Horn, a Swedish officer long familiar with UN operations, on this impossible mission. After a few whirling-dervish months without adequate support from UN headquarters, the Swede understandably blew his top and walked out. On October 30, 1963, the UN announced in effect that it was giving up on Yemen.

Fortuitously on the same day came an announcement of success in old-fashioned peace-making. Haile Selassie got Ben Bella and King Hassan II to sign a cease-fire agreement in their Algerian-Moroccan border war. The Emperor of Ethiopia's accomplishment was in instructive contrast to the efforts made under the charter.

Shortly after the Algerians and Moroccans began shooting at one another, the old Lion of Judah got into his jet and went to work shuttling between Rabat and Algiers. There was no ponderous convocation of the Security Council to deliberate, debate, misrepresent, accuse, recommend, abstain from, or veto action on a breach of the peace. Nor was there a gathering together of the General Assembly, a uniting for peace by a diverse and largely uninformed body of representatives having to refer back to 113 governments whether so to unite.

Haile Selassie immediately lined up President Keita of Mali as comediator. This was smart; one monarch and one Marxist, matching Hassan, a king, and Ben Bella, the socialist chum of Dr. Castro. The emperor then jetted to Paris for lunch with de Gaulle, to Belgrade for a talk with Tito, and to Cairo to advise Nasser that this was an African not an Arab quarrel and to keep his fishhooks out of these troubled waters.

Getting his cease-fire in a fortnight was an impressive

performance for the 225th consecutive Solomonic ruler, a man whom most of the world regarded as a picturesque anachronism. And the old-fashioned procedure of quiet good offices was off the ground and into operation before the new diplomacy of universal participation, committees, and task forces could have gotten sufficiently organized to be even officially cognizant of the problem.

The UN is not the bulwark against war that it is widely assumed to be. There has been no general war, not because of UN restraints but because of calculations of national self-interest. If these calculations were to change, the UN as such would be a trifling consideration in the decision reached.

The Washington-Moscow "hot line" does not run through U Thant's office. And were the UN to disappear from the scene, the world would no more plunge into a big war than it is likely to do with the world organization in existence.

The 1962 confrontation between the United States and the Soviet Union over Cuba confirmed this. Washington and Moscow worked out the clash between themselves. Neither could yield decisions regarding its vital security to any third party, least of all to the world organization. The UN was dragged into the affair after the crisis had passed its peak. All that happened as a result of this was its public humiliation by Castro.

The combination of Soviet intrigue against us and the irresponsibility of many of the new and disoriented countries does not augur well for international tranquillity. Stating a British view of the General Assembly in July, 1962, the then foreign secretary, Lord Home, said: "A small minority subscribe to what they know to be wrong and dangerous and ally themselves with the Communists to do us maximum harm; while altogether too many of their fellow members allow themselves to be swept along, reluctantly perhaps and somewhat shamefacedly, on this tide of malice."

Someday on some issue seriously affecting us we may find a majority of the UN aligned against us. This will be an unhappy awakening for us. It will be the end of our dream of sharing power on a vote-to-vote basis, of counting on our friendly example, counsel, and suasion to persuade others to vote for what was right and proper—what we stood for.

Finally, we seem to have acted in the belief that matters are advanced by ventilation, that somehow a good airing in the UN wind tunnel serves to improve the situation. This is a highly relative judgment, depending on how temperate and salubrious is the atmosphere in circulation.

The prudent course for us is to extend one on which we already seem to have embarked. It is to deemphasize the role that the UN plays in the conduct of American foreign relations. There is no need for fanfare in this. It is preferable that the change take place rather gradually. Abruptness is generally poor practice in foreign relations.

Little or no change need be made in our business with the International Court of Justice and the various specialized agencies such as the Food and Agricultural Organization and the World Bank. Most of them serve a useful purpose and should continue to receive our support so long as this is the case. Since they work within reasonably defined limitations, they do not suffer from the cosmic vapors that afflict the General Assembly, the Security Council, and political committees.

Where we have the diplomatic initiative, the change will not be great. Already many of the important substantive problems are dealt with outside the UN. An unhappy exception is nuclear weapons control and disarmament. Even so, when it came to practical negotiating—on the Partial Test Ban Agreement—it was the interested nuclear powers alone that dealt with the problem. U Thant was brought in at the signing ceremonies to be photographed and sip a glass of sticky Caucasian champagne. On such touchy matters as arms, the major powers have to work the problem out among themselves. Alcoholics Anonymous does not refer its cases to the WCTU for action.

As a stern rule, we should avoid introducing new issues into the UN unless it is clearly to our advantage to do so. This will not leave us isolated and unequipped to work for peace. Our enormous paraphernalia for the conduct of foreign relations should be able to do the job. In a practical sense the UN is one more layer of bureaucratic tissue through which communication has to drip.

In sum, what we can accomplish through the UN we can do at least as effectively and with less risk through traditional diplomatic procedure, although admittedly less spectacularly. Even the deals reportedly made in the corridors of the UN can by the same token be made in almost any other corridor, including that of a wagon-lits.

Essential in this shift of emphasis is that our public figures moderate their overblown pronouncements about the UN, for perhaps the saddest aspect of the UN is that it is the victim of the supersell.

Paul Bunyan and the United Nations

Like the Grand Design, the Alliance for Progress, and other respectable aspirations, it would have made sense had it been kept within reasonable bounds. But it and the others were given the Paul Bunyan treatment. They were described in hyperbole, as were the objectives of World War I—to make the world safe for democracy.

Perhaps it is necessary to overstate a decent and noble intent to get any reaction at all. Unhappily, such inspired promotion sometimes carries away a large part of the audience, thus compromising the objectives sought and complicating a rational approach to international affairs.

Of course the UN has a rightful place in the modern world, but at the present low stage of human social development, its place is not that to which it has been assigned and to which it now pretends. The realistic and constructive role of the Security Council, the General Assembly, and political committees is not operational. It is philosophic. Let these bodies debate the issues that set man against man. Let them pass resolutions and make recommendations. Let them make studies and issue reports. But do not let them overreach and so entangle themselves in the conduct of international relations.

Much good and little damage can come of this less pretentious function. Such a UN would be a public reminder that we are all members of the human family and that someday we needs must learn to order our affairs on earth, and off it, pretty much as vowed in the charter.

The debates and the studies by the world organization could meanwhile serve as a running commentary on where and why differences among us were widening and where and why we might be making headway toward agreement. Resolutions and recommendations would consciously be a rough measure of how far from or how close to unity we were in the present chaos of sovereign nation states. American and like-minded representatives could serve as public monitors of man's struggle toward international sanity.

These would be great and good accomplishments. But to attempt more may prove to be fatal.

The main thing is to keep alive some symbol of hope of a future world order as we and surely the next generation grope our primitive, frightful way through international anarchy.

Sharper Than
a Serpent's Tooth

*T*he Kremlin is struggling on four fronts. It is engaged in two cold wars, tactics of enticement, and a mopping-up campaign against internal enemy holdouts.

It has been losing both cold wars, is failing to allure, and is bogged down by stubborn, passive resistance in its domestic clean-up operations.

It has been losing the struggle to bring down its enemies, the United States and Western Europe. It has also been losing the other cold war—against its ally, Peking. Nor has it been captivating the underdeveloped countries. Finally, against its own people, it has yet to win over the passive resistance of the unreconstructed.

The course of the conflict against us may be reversed and the Kremlin may finally triumph. But this could happen only if the U.S.S.R. successfully exploited an invulnerable military advantage over us, or we betray ourselves.

The neocolonial attempt of the Soviet rulers to subjugate China and deny it its ideological and organizational independence goes back to the early twenties. From time to time it has seemed to succeed, but in the end, Moscow will lose. It probably already has.

As for the so-called emergent countries, they have been mostly disabused of their illusions. Some may yet succumb if, in mismanaging their own affairs, they lay themselves open to Soviet subversion.

With its own people, it is a process familiar in history. The invading horde or faith conquers and transforms. At the same time the realities of the environment and of human nature transform the invader. It may take decades or it may take centuries, but it is inevitable. Having conquered with Marxism-Leninism it is now the Kremlin's turn to be frustrated and slowly changed by those whom it has subdued.

All these things can be so or come to fruition only, of course, if there is no nuclear war.

The Kremlin does not admit, cannot admit, that it is losing. It believes that it is riding the tidal force of history, on which it will triumph. It views domestic opposition as a vestigial or aberrant manifestation that is manageable.

The heterodoxy of the fraternal Chinese is more dramatic, but at least they are Marxists, joined with the Bolsheviks in a common hostility to the Imperialist West.

And the emergent countries, as seen from the Kremlin, are ripening for take-over by either Moscow or Peking.

It is in looking at what happened to the West after World War II that the Kremlin finds reason for optimism. Before the war, it had been socialism in one country, the U.S.S.R. Now one-third of the people of the world are in the "socialist camp."

In the Kremlin's view the West let this happen. It let a war-crippled Soviet Union take Eastern Europe. In the United States the executive, abetted by Congress and the public, demobilized pell-mell on the heels of the war. The Americans sought a political compromise rather than an imposed military decision favorable to the Nationalists in the gigantic convulsion of the Chinese revolution. That serious intervention in China—which would have meant another war of indefinite dimensions and duration—was something that the American people would not have countenanced is an explanation that the Kremlin regards as simply further evidence of American decadence.

When it had an atomic monopoly the United States failed (incredibly to the rulers of Russia) to force a nuclear neutralization of the Soviet Union. Instead it did nothing, while the U.S.S.R. developed a nuclear potential that has grown to challenge that of the United States.

More recently the Americans permitted Castroism to become established and grow, and then allowed the Russians to move into and settle down on Cuba, close upon their exposed southeastern flank. Only when the U.S.S.R. introduced "offensive" weapons onto the island did Washington force a showdown. But in the clinch, Washington faltered at compelling the Russians to pack up their "defensive" weapons and leave the island.

To the Kremlin, this was decadent funk. To the Soviet rulers, it bore out what the Marxist-Leninist "science of history" predicted—the rottenness of imperialism. Yet if we should force the removal of their legions and the overthrow of Castro, this, too, would be in accordance with their book. They would categorize it as a desperate lashing out of imperialism in its last throes.

The texts of Marxism-Leninism are so profuse and sometimes contradictory that they can be selectively drawn upon to explain almost any situation and justify any tactic. Thus preoccupation with these scriptures as a clue to Soviet behavior can end up in scholasticism and befuddlement.

Communism is a faith. Like others before it, the real driving force is an emotional commitment to a basically simple idea.

The idea is that all life is a conflict between that which is dying and bad and that which is emerging and good. That which is dying and bad will, sooner or later, be destroyed by that which is emerging and good. That which is emerging and good is sure to prevail, sooner or later. This is foreordained by Science.

For Science is God. Marx and Lenin were the true Prophets. Mao has promoted himself to their company as a living Prophet Emeritus. Khrushchev, insisting that Mao is a false prophet, contents himself for the time being with the status of Caliph of Muscovy. Mao, however, proclaims that Khrushchev has betrayed the teachings of the true prophets. But both share a faith in the truth of dialectical materialism, as revealed by Science to Marx and Lenin.

The essence of truth is the clash between what is dying and what is aborning. There is conflict, there is violence, because that which must go resists to the last its demise and that which will be fights to become. There is no such thing as harmonious evolution or mutually beneficial compromise.

And tolerance is a mortal sin.

It is the duty, the privilege, and the glory of the individual Communist to help history be fulfilled, to be a militant part of the inevitable process. If one cannot be the driver of the locomotive of history, at least one may be one of the crew.

To participate in this great endeavor one must have a compulsion to destroy. The emergent, the good, cannot be realized until the dying, the bad, has been crushed. The motor emotion is hate. Only thus is communist dynamism generated.

To hate is virtuous when directed at whatever resists the emergence of the new. It is not only morally praiseworthy; it is "progressive." Hence it follows that all practical expressions of this animosity are permissible, even laudable— from war and murder to petty deceptions.

Other faiths have been motivated by love or fear or a yearning for immortality. Even Islam, with its holy wars and death to the unbeliever, tolerated dissent if tribute was paid. But Marxism-Leninism is implacable.

The vision of an ultimate utopian communist society has drawn many to the movement, but if the convert cannot persist in active hate and accept discipline, he becomes disillusioned and is, in one fashion or another, discarded.

For Utopia, with its classless society, its withered-away state, no one misbehaving, no cops and no robbers, is still far off. Even the Soviet Union admits that it is still in the stage of constructing communism.

In this transitional phase where the U.S.S.R. now is, the doctrine asserts that not all is creative, bringing into existence the new. The Old Nick of capitalist remnants in the Soviet

Union persists and must be extirpated. These bourgeois vestiges and the backsliding of the new, made-in-U.S.S.R. generation excite the hostility of the faithful and engage a large share of the Communist party's efforts. Thus hate is an active force in the Kremlin's relations with its own people as well as with foreigners.

In a basic sense, then, the Kremlin is alone against the world. It is struggling against its enemies to the west, its prey to the south, its allies to the east, and its subjects within.

It is the struggle within the Soviet Union that is crucial for the Kremlin, for the U.S.S.R. is its power base. As such it is the most sensitive, the most vital area of the Kremlin's power anatomy. Because the rulers of Russia came to power through conspiracy and subversion, because they reign not by reference to popular will but by writ, wile, and repression, and because they claim to embody infallible truth and the hope of mankind, they are morbidly concerned with the Soviet people.

How did this all come about?

Marxism was alien to the Russians. The Bolsheviks, a small underground conspiracy, imposed upon the Russians a Western idea from a German theoretician out of England. It was as foreign to the masses as the importations of Peter the Great.

Lenin Russified this alien concept. He blended it operationally with the worst of the Slavic heritage—cunning, violence, tyranny, retreat before superior force, and merciless subjugation of lesser force. He added something peculiarly his own. It was an uncanny insight into and a consuming concern with organizing, disciplining, and manipulating masses of people.

While Lenin amplified and particularized Marx's ideology, it was his formulas for the practical application of communist theory that were his most significant contribution to the movement. Lenin's evil genius created two formulas, one for the seizure of power (as practiced in the October Revolution) and the other for the maintenance in power of the Bolshevik oligarchy (through a combination of an infallible ideology and a totalitarian party-state apparatus).

Stalin inherited this system and, having an unusually low opinion of his fellow men, exercised discipline with even more stringency than Lenin.

In his turn Khrushchev recognized that a certain spontaneity—a quality in which he himself has not been deficient—was necessary in the Soviet people if they were to outperform "capitalist slaves." He has therefore been somewhat more relaxed.

This does not mean that Khrushchev has abandoned the labor of Lenin and Stalin to bring about the creation of that synthetic personality—Soviet man. Soviet man is the idealized citizen needed by the Kremlin to uphold the absolutism of the Kremlin.

Certainly Soviet man is unique in the varied explanations of the origin of man. According to his creators, he did not, like Cro-Magnon and the rest of us, emerge out of the Garden of Eden. Nor is he the descendant of anyone out of the steamy past. Rather, like Minerva, Soviet man springs forth full-blown. In this case, it is from the head of Science.

Soviet man is the child of Science, the Marxist-Leninist God. Science was applied systematically to create this synthetic creature. The origins were thus.

Historical, political, economic, sociological, and psychological principles, as understood in the West, were altered to conform to and serve the master science of Marxism-Leninism. In matters concerning man and society, the "scientific" revelations of Marx and Lenin were transmuted to dogma. Inspired interpretations usurped experimentation and infallibility replaced skepticism. Man the ruler used pseudo-science according to convenient interpretation to exploit man in the mass.

Science was applied systematically to produce this ersatz human being—Soviet man. This was attempted, preferably, through persuasion and Pavlovian conditioning, for totalitarianism, unlike the tyrannies of old which sought at most the imposition of slavery, demands more than submission. Soviet totalitarianism requires of the individual affirmative allegiance to the ideology, and if not conversion, at least conformity. For nonconformity there was "comradely" suasion, then coercion, and ultimately liquidation.

The U.S.S.R. has been a vast brainwashing establishment. While the urban American is said to be lathered with some sixteen hundred messages per day urging him to consume and be happy, Soviet man is soaked and scrubbed in stimuli —at labor, at rest, and at play—pressing him to salvation through Marxist-Leninist works and beliefs. And except for rare and restricted visits by such as Benny Goodman and the Archbishop of Canterbury, all contrary excitations are excluded.

It can scarcely be said that Soviet man is adrift in Soviet society. He is not allowed to be so. He is made to belong.

His are not the disorders arising out of permissiveness and indulgence. It is inadmissible that he should develop the spectator's outlook, least of all about himself. Aggressively he is told that he is a participant in the creation of a new world, and that therein must lie his greatest fulfillment.

Yet it is doubtful that Soviet man is an integrated personality. It is not that he has been denied liberty as we knew it. He has never had it; for him it is an abstraction. It is, probably, that he misses three things: natural human associations, the enjoyment of open curiosity, and the mysteries.

The undermining of human relationships in this "scientific" society tends to deplete the personality of Soviet man. The prerevolutionary Russian personality was robustly gregarious, emotional, and family centered. This was unlikely stuff out of which to make a collectivist state which, by its character, was jealous of all human attachments—friend to friend, brother to brother, husband to wife, child to parent. The state strove to sabotage these natural ties, accelerating and surpassing the disintegrating influence of industrialization.

It succeeded in the Stalin era to the point that basic social cohesion was endangered, damaging to the collectivist goal. The wrecking tactics have been eased. The party speaks even tenderly of the family. A less caustic brainwashing continues, but it still holds out as more worthy to be in love with a piece of state property, especially if one is a lady tractor driver, than with one's betrothed.

The exercise of curiosity is probably another lack in the Soviet personality. The normal desire to know is selectively repressed. Not only are some areas blank in Soviet man's knowledge, because information is kept from him, but he is also given to understand that to inquire into certain matters is risky.

Curiosity is nevertheless alive and becomes evident in periods of relaxed controls. It is, to us, a lopsided curiosity because of its frustrations and gaps.

The denial of the mysteries must be keenly felt by many, for the Russian soul had a broad streak of mysticism. The human spirit, life after death, divine power, and apprehension of deeper truths are "antiscientific" and therefore proscribed. They are not viewed, as in the West, as nonscientific, questions on which scientific opinion is in abeyance, or at most tentatively negative, and meanwhile the individual may believe in both scientific and spiritual truths.

The flat denial of the mysteries left an empty place in the personality of Soviet man. Hence it is not surprising to hear that some Russians at least are asking, as did their grandfathers, "But what is truth?"

The problem for the Kremlin is that Soviet man has not turned out in accordance with the Marxist-Leninist "scientific" plan. It now has a generation brought up without contaminating bourgeois contact. This conditioned generation should be selflessly dedicated to the communist cause and abide by the 1961 party program's moral code, including "conscientious labor for the good of society."

Each member of it should also display "an uncompromising attitude to injustice, parasitism, dishonesty, and careerism." Moreover, he is bound to exemplify "honesty and truthfulness, moral purity, modesty, and guilelessness in social and private life." All this should be summed up in an atheistic YMCA ideal man "who will harmoniously combine spiritual wealth, moral purity, and a perfect physique."

Naturally none of this has happened, is happening, or is likely to happen. Soviet man is bogged down with a full human share of anxieties, selfishness, dishonesty, and guile. These take forms somewhat different from ours, but they are there.

Boredom, cynicism, and careerism seem to affect most of the new generation's privileged class, the sons and daughters of party bosses and high military officers. They are the ones whose parents were able to get them into the best schools and launched in favored positions. They existed even back in Stalin's day right after the war. These young people are scarcely models of the party program's moral code, but there they are, high in communist society, ideological conformists or cynics, some of them parasites and many of them shrewdly able careerists.

All this, perhaps, the Kremlin could put up with as the wild oats of its own progeny. Also serious is the boredom of the unprivileged—and their continuing concern with self. The burning faith in the communist way of life and the enthusiasm for socialist construction are scarcely there.

To be sure, Soviet man lines up and says the right things when summoned by the gong, but that is his public, collective self. There also is his private self: withdrawn, skeptical, and resistant to the demands upon him. So Soviet man is a split personality without a split-level.

He may have the Ikelike Gagarin grin; he may be shown with it, puddling iron or with a sheaf of wheat clutched to the chest, never obscuring his medal as a Hero of Soviet

Labor. With all this he must still be a disappointment—except to the propaganda photographers, for with the Bolsheviks, too, the image is important.

Image without performance is, of course, not good enough. Performance under Stalin was extracted by invocation of faith and by knout. Khrushchev was perceptive enough to realize that times were changing and that to get more out of the Soviet people there had to be some relaxation of repression, some incentives, some loosening of the ideological bonds.

His first venture in easing the Stalinist terror brought on the Hungarian uprisings and ructions in Poland. He crushed the Hungarian revolt in Stalinesque fashion.

In the Soviet Union, writers were allowed to dwell on the iniquities of the Stalin era, until they touched an open nerve—did those who remained silent as Stalin perpetrated his crimes bear the guilt of acquiescence? Khrushchev, abristle with righteous indignation, in March, 1963, implausibly proclaimed that he had not known that innocent people had been victimized by his former boss and that discussion of what went on under Stalin was "a very dangerous theme." The controls were clamped back on.

This highlights the dilemma of relaxation versus repression. Permit even a little spontaneity and inquiry in a totalitarian regime and you risk getting antiparty tendencies.

For the Kremlin, literature is perhaps the most perilous area in which to loosen controls. Literature is the breeder and carrier of ideas to the masses, as the Bolsheviks well know from their successful underground past. Here a little contagion can start an epidemic.

In another area there has been a tempering of the ideological restrictions. This was in the physical sciences in which even in Stalin's time there was occasionally permitted a wider latitude of inquiry than elsewhere, for the economic and military advancement of the U.S.S.R. depended on scientific progress, and science could not progress if it was suffocated by ideology and an overlay of meddling party ignoramuses.

This license bothers the Kremlin. The authoritative 1961 Program of the Party lists as pressing a rationalization of the ideologically shady goings-on in the physical sciences. "In the age of rapid scientific progress," according to the anxious words of the program, "the elaboration of the philosophical problems of modern natural science on the basis of dialectical materialism, the only scientific world outlook and method of cognition, becomes still more important."

Unable to keep its hands off, the party is determined to bend authentic science to Marxism-Leninism. This promises to be quite an undertaking. It can hardly turn out other than frustrating to the dogmatists, and meanwhile galling to the scientists. It raises the question of what the Kremlin would do were the scientists—a vitally important segment of Soviet society—to become a serious source of ideological infection. Which would the rulers do: let the infection spread and risk a domestic plague, or sterilize the scientists and risk impotence abroad?

The strongest support for sterilization comes from the party's apparatchiks and the government's bureaucrats. They are in favor of cracking down on the slightest heterodoxy. They are uneasy over the slight concessions that have been made, for they have a vested interest in communist conventionality, as they learned it for many years under Stalin. They are against innovations, rocking the boat. They are probably the strongest influence for Bolshevik fundamentalism.

Khrushchev brought to the upper levels of the party some of the younger apparatchiks. However vigorous and ventursome they may be, they are still party men who will assumably resist any move that would undermine or weaken the authority of the apparatus that gives them status and in which they hope to rise and shine. They may be much less imbued with the faith, but they are no less concerned with the perpetuation of the power structure of which they are a part.

There is, then, a broad and deep inner conflict inside Soviet society. On one side is the reactionary element of the party, tending to restrict creativity and growth by means of repression, by jealous monitoring of human behavior—even the human condition—and by imposition of a doctrine overtaken by history. On the other side are the Soviet people, most of them passively resistant, with a wide range of urges and wants, from a longing for free inquiry and expression among the creative minds to the collective farmer's desire to profit more from his labor and the state farmer's hankering for a home-cooked supper away from the communal mess hall.

The contradiction is clearly seen in the case of agriculture. The doctrine is that agriculture must be collectivized or state owned. The reality is that the kolkhoz and the state farm are relatively unproductive. Even so the Russians did not go to the lengths of the Chinese ideological idiocy—communes. The dogma-imposed and apparatchik-maintained collectives have consistently been a sufficient fiasco.

Deprived of incentives, the peasant, always and everywhere a peculiarly stubborn fellow, has effectively played the sly oaf. And the vast, low-grade legions of functionaries for farm management and for collecting and distributing foodstuffs have far overfulfilled their norm of incompetence, boneheadedness, crookedness, and sloth.

The Kremlin is, of course, not oblivious to these and other contradictions across the panorama of the Soviet system, but it can do little else than follow the line dictated by the faith.

For the Marxist-Leninist opiate of the people is also the opiate of the bosses. However they may creatively interpret and extend the doctrine, they are still addicts. They cannot after some fifty years of ideological dope break off suddenly—or perhaps even gradually.

Even were the rulers of the Kremlin to become disabused of their faith, they would not publicly renounce communism. Rare individuals might, but only as fugitive apostates. Most would, with covert cynicism, abide by doctrine and liturgy if for no other reason than that the ideology and its now established practices give "legitimacy" to their assertion of authority over their fellow men. From no other source—not from divine right, not line of succession, not democratic choice—can they claim sanction to rule.

Having a sneaking guilty conscience, a secret yen for respectability, and pretensions to being messianic for all humanity, the men in the Kremlin cannot be satisfied with the otherwise acceptable position of a junta, originally come to power by coup d'état, in which succession is determined by quite uncomradely scheming and disguised or legalized assassinations. There is plenty of precedent for this, but it is not good enough for the dictators of the proletariat.

In addition to providing a cloak of legitimacy for these latter-day tyrants, the infallible writ of Marxism-Leninism serves to justify suppression and other excesses used to enforce totalitarianism. The wrong that is done is made right by citations of doctrine. This is elastically convenient. Moreover, it is the only way that the Kremlin knows how to govern.

Were the rest of the world to stand still, were Moscow somehow able miraculously to withdraw the Soviet Union from the international scene, in theory the Kremlin might be able to concentrate on resolving in one fashion or another the inner contradictions of the Soviet system. But of course this is not the case. The U.S.S.R. is living in, as the Bolsheviks say, a system of states in which it chooses, because of its nature and its faith, to be in frenetic competition with the United States.

This competition intensifies the internal contradictions. The need of broad, rapid economic development to approach the American level requires a relaxation of thought control to engender creativity and some degree of popular enthusiasm for the growth effort.

But in conflict with economic advance across the board are the enormous needs of the arms and space races. There is not enough for an all-out effort on both fronts. Resources are therefore diverted from civilian and earthbound needs to the power programs that put butter on nobody's table.

The results of this are, if not restiveness requiring repressions, then negativism and cynicism, which goads the apparatchiks to hip-hip-hooray agitation. This in turn grates on Soviet man, who cannot even have marmalade instead.

But even were there no arms race, were the competition not only peaceful but also demilitarized, there would still be chills running up and down the spines of the apparatchiks and their bosses in the Kremlin over any relaxation, over any welling up of spontaneity. Could they control a really spontaneous demonstration of popular enthusiasm? The inclination would be to react according to their conditioning.

Soviet man is thus inevitably low man on the Kremlin totem. For in the ultimate analysis, if the Kremlin had to choose between creative growth through relaxation, jeopardizing its authority, and stagnation from repression, it would retreat to its core concern—control of the Soviet people—and choose stagnation.

Even were it to win the world—and the moon and space —what would it profit the Kremlin were it to lose in the process domination over its base of power?

The rulers of Russia will, naturally, strive to avoid so stark and disastrous a choice. They will continue to vacillate, now repressive, now relaxing a little, expecting that somehow or other the future will work out as Science and the Prophets predicted.

There is one prediction of the Prophets that they do not wish to see fulfilled—an apocalyptic war. Unless the U.S.S.R. devises an impregnable defense, such a clash in a world of weapons of mass destruction carries an unacceptable risk to the Kremlin's power base. Therefore, so long as this situation exists, and the men who rule Russia are sane, they will avoid expanding local conflicts into general war.

If we keep ahead in the arms race, if we refrain from so challenging the Kremlin's vital security that it is forced to war—and if it does not dementedly lash out against us—then what might the future hold within the Soviet Union?

A great deal depends upon the pace that we set in the arms and space races. If we pull well ahead, the Kremlin may overstrain its civilian economy in an attempt to catch up. This might lead to serious friction between the rulers and the ruled, the nature and outcome of which are unpredictable.

Assuming that civilian wants are not markedly depressed, rather that life slowly betters, it is unlikely that Soviet man will become more ideologically motivated, as the party program predicts. It is more likely that the faith will become more of a formality than it is now. Some may privately scoff, but most will accept it as a convention and go through the motions of the Bolshevik liturgy but privately lead their own lives.

Under these conditions an uprising of the people against the tyrants seems improbable. And even were there a successful revolution, the new regime would probably resemble more the present one than any Western democracy, for the Soviet people are now so conditioned to "socialism" that they would want at most the reform, not the overthrow, of Marxism-Lenism. Any idea that they would welcome liberation by foreigners is farfetched. Soviet patriotism is so strong that among many it amounts to chauvinism.

Quite possibly, the strongest pressure toward collectivization and conformity in the Soviet Union is now not ideology but industrialization. Advancing industrialization in the West increasingly agglomerates and regiments people. The same process is at work in the U.S.S.R., irrespective of communist ideology.

The same impersonal force presses on the Kremlin. In one sense, obviously, industrialization suits Marxist-Leninist theory. In another it does not, for industrialization is supremely pragmatic, while Marxism-Leninism, notwithstanding its flexibility, is essentially dogmatic.

If the Kremlin does not repress the Soviet Union into stagnation or collapse, but vacillates toward the Bolshevik dream of industrialization, in the process the Kremlin itself will be slowly changed. The younger men who know how to manage, contribute to, and make work a highly industrialized system will, of necessity, come increasingly to the fore: administrators who understand the productive complex, scientists, and highly specialized technicians. Neither these more creative minds nor computers are ideologically imbued.

This upcoming situation is not the old Stalinist frontier industrialization: here a dam, there a railroad, yonder a metallurgical center. As we know, it is something far more complicated, interdependent, and delicate than that which those who are now the old fogies of the party crudely dealt with. Their control in the future could turn out to be disastrous for the Kremlin.

With the educated, fact-seeking, fact-demanding new generation coming, initially not to power but to much greater influence, the Khrushchev or post-Khrushchev Kremlin can repress them only at the peril of industrial shambles. And if it allows them their pragmatic way, the faith will be further eroded. Reality will wear down fanaticism.

The rising generation—and the next to follow—may not make the world safer for democracy, for "great-power chauvinism," as the Chinese call it, may come to supplant conspiratorial dedication to revolution. If there is a gain for peace, an advance toward a live-and-let-live relationship, it will be perhaps in a lessening of unintelligibility out of Moscow.

As science, technology, and industrialization crowd us in the West under increasing control by the state, they paradoxically tend to loosen the rigid bonds of totalitarianism. Thus we come closer together in experience and outlook and ease of communication. Hence that which creates the weapons whereby we may all be consumed may yet produce some sort of understanding and possibly even give rise to a certain tolerance.

The real threat to the Bolsheviks in the Kremlin is not imperialism in its last throes nor the heresies of fraternal parties nor the Russian masses whom they have so abused but the new Soviet elite which they have nurtured—their own serpent-toothed sons.

The
Other Cold War

*C*hina is a surging human sea and the rest of us Canutes vainly bidding the rising tide to stay. This is one view of Communist China.

From their rich but sparsely peopled expanse the Russians watch with foreboding across a long, sullen border the stirrings of the growing Chinese horde. With supple fatalism, soft Southeast Asia awaits the swarming mass it feels powerless to withstand. And India, peering up into the Himalayas, sees the abominable Chinaman descending upon its open plains.

Even we behind two oceans and our stockade of missiles and plans for antimissile missiles sometimes wonder what the inventors of pyrotechnics may ultimately visit upon the rest of mankind.

The other view of China, at the opposite extreme, is that the Mao Dynasty has already exhausted the mandate of Heaven. By this interpretation, the Chinese people will have eaten of so much bitterness—and little else—and the Forbidden City will have been so foiled in trying to remake the nature of China that the tyrants will be overcome. Revolt may rise from within the Politburo Palace. Or it may burst forth from a barracks.

The truth is that what will happen in China during even the next decade is a mystery. It is a somber mystery, auguring little hopeful, boding many afflictions.

Nowhere else are the dimensions of uncertainty greater. It is not so much the 700 million people nor the 3,750,000 square miles of mountains, deserts, and fertile plains; it is more the magnitude and suddenness of the change demanded of the 700 million and their environment.

While Confucianism and the hierarchical, centralized structure of Chinese society were in some respects adaptable to Marxism-Leninism, the attempts of the party and the state to usurp the roles of patriarch, father, and elder brother of every Chinese have had a shattering effect. The communist dictatorship so intended it. The revolutionary rulers were determined to destroy their rival, the family system, the core of Chinese society and conservatism.

This wrecking of the family system was not done gradually. Immediately after seizing power, the new regime rushed to impose the intimate supremacy of the party-state over every man, woman, and child. To what extent it has succeeded cannot be gauged until the post-1950 generation has reached maturity. Those born before mid-century had been conditioned by the family system.

Any totalitarian regime, of course, regards the older generation as close to incorrigible and in any event expendable. It is to be intimidated and used, and, if not usable, discarded. The hopes of the dictatorship are set on the new generation, ideologically conditioned from infancy.

The Chinese revolution, still aggressively fanatic, has differed from the Russian one during its dynamic youth. It is different in the sheer human mass to be made over. It is so in the limited natural resources of China, in contrast to the abundant endowment of the Soviet Union. It differs also in that the Russian revolution came first and that Peking is striving, under more difficult circumstances, to catch up to and someday surpass what the Kremlin has accomplished. In a sense the Forbidden City feels more alone in its incredible undertaking—and hence more desperate—than even the Bolsheviks did because, although part of a camp of fraternal socialist states, it is scorned and put upon by its revolutionary elder.

Hence the combination of vaulting ambition and maddening frustration fans the fanaticism of the rulers of China.

They are an extraordinary collection, the men who created and now uphold the Mao Dynasty. For decades they have worked together. It was only four years after Lenin's death and two before Stalin consolidated his supremacy that Mao set up, in 1927, the first Chinese Communist government. To be sure, it was over only a few villages, it was temporary, and it was fugitive. But it was the first of several larger ones until, in 1935, a base area administration was established in Northwest China. However small and precarious the beginnings, Mao and his comrades experienced more than two decades of governing villages, towns, and counties before they captured national power in 1950.

These shrewd, disciplined, relentless young intellectuals —most of them from well-to-do families—learned not only how to rule from the rice roots up. They were also tested and hardened in the 5,000-mile ordeal of the Long March, in the patient lying low of the war years in Yenan, and in the sly, agile maneuvers of survival and growth behind the Japanese lines during World War II.

In those years of proving, the fainthearted and the recalcitrant fell by the wayside, got out or were ousted.

The remainder stuck together and now rule China. They have maintained group solidarity on through revolutionary victory and established power. Since taking over, they have had a few discreet liquidations and demotions in the oligarchy, but the Forbidden City has undergone nothing like the series of unsightly, unsettling purges and scrambles for succession that have more than once demoralized the Kremlin.

The relative stability of the Chinese dictatorship exists largely because Mao confirmed and confidently maintained his supremacy for three decades, achieving finally the status of Sage–Clausewitz–Son of Heaven. His acknowledged preeminence has created a situation of stability in which he has held his subordinates together after his own image.

When Mao, the founder of the dynasty, goes, or if he falters—what then? The historic dynastic succession was by primogeniture. Under a rule by democratic centralism, uncertainty swirls in.

Unattracted by the discomposure of the Russians in these matters, Mao appears to have tried to place the intoxicating issue of succession out of reach. Liu Shao-chi, the president, seems to occupy second place in the hierarchy, distinctly a cut above everyone else.

It does not necessarily follow, however, that with the passing of Mao, this dour zealot is certain to take over. Mao may propose, but without his commanding presence, temptations and opportunities to dispose otherwise may become irresistible.

Democratic centralism in the ruling group may function in ideological and operational issues, the boss casting the decisive vote, but with the boss gone and the issue being who the next boss is to be, the decisive vote may be forced through by the strongest, the most resolute, and the craftiest. In democratic centralism, succession, not being by blood, tends to end up in blood.

Whoever the successor to Mao, he will probably be one of the ingrown, provincial bigots of the ruling group. With the exception of Chou En-lai, the members of the Politburo are essentially unacquainted with the contemporary noncommunist world. And the intelligence that they receive from abroad is almost surely ideologically filtered.

This partial and distorted understanding of countries outside the socialist camp is of course typical of most communist ruling circles throughout the world. And in the game of international blindman's buff, the reverse is also true. But with the Chinese, the phenomenon of blind spots and myopia is particularly pronounced.

To begin with, they are scarcely less ethnocentric than their fathers. The Middle Kingdom mentality of their progenitors revolved around Confucianism, ancestor worship, Chinese cultural superiority, and although seldom articulated, racial supremacy. All others were barbarians and, in the case of the white man, hairy and with an offensive body odor.

The Red Mandarinate is no less haughty about the superiority of Marxism-Maoism. All others, except the ideological tribute bearers, are revisionists or they are imperialists and their running dogs.

The Chinese Politburo's vision is circumscribed also by a quarter of a century of fugitive seclusion. The back-country life, the sticky submersion in the peasantry, the holing up in the Shensi badlands, all of these threw them back, inward-looking, upon themselves.

When they finally came to power they established their capital at Peking, which, under the Mongol emperors, our ancestors called Cambaluc. Suddenly the horizon widened out over the encampments of socialism, stretching across the steppelands of Eurasia to East Germany and the Balkans. This, though not all of the world, was all of the world that Kublai and his fellow Khans knew. The Chinese warmed to the hospitality of the other Marxist chieftains.

But this expansive sense of association was before long rebuffed. For full reasons of their own, the Russians closed, so far as they could, the opening to the wider fraternity. The arrogant, naïve Chinese were forced back once again upon themselves. For those so proudly emerging from insignificance, this was an infuriating turn.

The Chinese had reason out of their past to scorn and detest the Russians. Now, humiliated by the big noses, as, in their more tolerant moods, they called their predecessors in Marxism, scorned as ideologically impetuous and immature, and deprived of aid which they felt to be their proper due, they nourished a passionate resentment against Moscow.

Both the Chinese and the Russians have long memories of one another. And there is much to remember.

They had both been conquered by the Mongols. But the Chinese, with a civilization superior to that of their conquerors, had taught, finally absorbed, and, in so doing, corrupted their alien rulers. The Russians, in contrast, were treated as vassals by the barbarian horsemen and instructed by them in civil administration, a knowledge of which the Golden Horde had acquired from the Chinese. It was from China that the Russians got a census, a postal system, and an indoctrination in submission to centralized, autocratic authority.

Ghenghis Khan had in 1214 done a thorough piece of Mongol city planning on the Chinese capital: sacked it, burned it, and massacred all the inhabitants. His grandson Kublai built on the blighted site Cambaluc and to it, from Karakorum, moved the capital of the Mongol Empire. Thereby, in a sense, the Mongol Empire was absorbed by that which it had conquered, the Chinese Empire.

The Mongol Dynasty of the Chinese Empire expanded eastward to conquer Korea and southward to subdue Burma and what is now Vietnam. Suzerainty was established over Tibet without even an invasion.

After Kublai the dynasty became progressively more Chinese. Tiled palaces replaced yurts. No longer lashing Mongol ponies at a gallop across the grasslands of Eurasia, the scourges of two continents reclined on the silks of palanquins, borne to an artificial hill raised within an artificial sea. The quaffing of fermented mare's milk had become non-upper-class; sips of tepid rice wine were the custom. And by the fourteenth century there was a contingent of rude Russian soldiery in the Chinese Imperial Guard.

The rhythm of Chinese history had passed from the phase of barbarian infusion and restless, expanding vitality to the phase of sedentary, introspective, conservative refinement—and decay.

But as the Chinese went through the Indian summer of the subsequent Ming Dynasty, there was stirring in Russia the surge to the Pacific. By the sixteenth century, Russian great-power chauvinism, as the descendants of the Mings are now pleased to term it, was on the march. The Slavic conquest of Siberia, the winning of the golden east, had begun. It turned out to be no less adventurous and bloody than that which was just beginning on the North American continent. In one case the pioneer was scalped by the aborigines; in the other his tongue was cut out by his own kind and he was exiled to the involuntary role of backwoodsman.

It was not until the seventeenth century that the Russian *Drang nach Osten* clashed with the Chinese. This occurred with the first Cossack incursions into the rich Amur valley of northern Manchuria. Pushing out of the incredibly dreary forests and mountains of the north, these freebooters boated and rafted down the great river—fighting the tribes that they encountered—and established a fortified settlement. Now this was territory that the new, virile Manchu Dynasty at Peking claimed, even though its nature and extent were unknown to the Celestial Court, not yet on the slow but certain course of decadence.

Peking reacted to this Slavic intrusion. Twice Manchu troops routed the Russian settlers and burned to the ground

Albazin, their fortified village on the Amur. For a third time the Siberians rebuilt their fortifications, and then withstood the siege.

The Russian court was going through one of its periodic convulsions over the succession to the throne, in which was involved in this instance a child who was to become Peter the Great. In any event Moscow wanted no additional complications in Asia. It had enough in Europe. So it sought a tranquilization on the remote frontiers with the Manchus.

Hence near the drear little Siberian town of Nerchinsk, in 1689, a pompous Chinese delegation accompanied by two Jesuit interpreters-counselors met with an ostentatious Russian delegation which had spent two years getting from Moscow to the conference site. The Manchu prince blandly proposed that the boundary be the Lena River. This would have given the Chinese all of eastern Siberia to the Arctic and Pacific Oceans.

The Russians quickly rejected the proposal. The Chinese then insisted on the entire Amur valley and its tributary, the Shilka, to Nerchinsk. The Russians still resisted. While the bargaining continued for three weeks, a Manchu army of foot soldiers and cavalry moved to deny the Russian envoy a dignified withdrawal from those awkward parleys and to threaten Nerchinsk. This was persuasive.

The plenipotentiary of the czar hastily yielded the Amur, accepted the watershed north of the river, and compromised on the line to the west. This was confirmed in the Treaty of Nerchinsk, in Chinese, Russian, and Latin. With minor revisions, subsequently negotiated, this pact was pretty much respected for nearly 170 years, by way of being a record as treaties go.

There was little cause for friction between China and Russia during this period. The Russians were absorbed in the exploration of the vast unknowns of northeastern Siberia, Kamchatka, Alaska—even California and Hawaii. For the Manchu Dynasty, its problems lay to the south of the Great Wall, where the Celestial sway came to be increasingly bedeviled by the seaborne barbarians from Europe and America.

Chinese defeats by the English in the first Anglo-Chinese War (1840–42) evoked a strategic concept, attributed to the imperial high commissioner at Canton, which bore the brunt of the English onslaught:

> To keep on the defensive would, therefore, prove to be our ruin. . . . We did not act thus when the treaty was concluded with Russia; for instead of waiting for the arrival of their forces, we became ourselves the aggressors, and then forever inspired fear and respect for our Empire. Hence our northwestern frontier has never been disturbed, and we retain our ascendancy in Tartary. . . .
>
> The Russians are now our friends; their territory is not very far from the English, and joins ours. We should therefore spend thirty million taels in raising a daring army, and march directly through the Russian country to England. . . . Since the Russians are the enemies of the English, they would support our undertaking, finding for us, on our arrival in their country, guns and furnishing us with auxiliaries.

This wily grand strategy, like many war plans since, was fortunately, for its author, never put to the test. The English and the French continued to humiliate China militarily. And the Russians chose to become scavengers of China's transition to modernity.

Doing it the hard way, in 1860 the British and the French, with some sixteen thousand troops, fought their way into Peking. Coincidentally, a Russian envoy, twenty-eight-year-old General Ignatiev, with fourteen Cossacks eased into the imperial capital as a friend of both sides. The unhappy Prince Kung, left behind by a craven and befuddled emperor to cope with the barbarians, turned to Ignatiev for sympathetic Russian advice.

The young general counseled that the allied demands be immediately accepted. This would forestall what the allies did not intend but what the Manchu court feared from memory of its own and Mongol invasions—the uprooting of the dynasty and the conquest of the empire. But even if the amphibious red-haired devils were placated by acceptance of their really not excessive demands, there still remained the dismaying prospect of permanent foreign occupation of Peking.

This even less substantial apprehension was so lively in the Manchu mind that the solicitous Ignatiev assured Prince Kung that he would exercise his influential good offices with the allied emissaries, Lord Elgin and Baron Gros, to persuade them to do what the Russian knew they would do without his intercession: withdraw their forces after Chinese submission to the allied terms. In appreciation of saving the dynasty from the burden and humiliation of indefinite foreign occupation and in the spirit of Russo-Chinese amity, Ignatiev indicated that it would be appropriate for China to cede to

Russia some wasteland in the far, bleak north, frequented only by bandits and tigers. With grateful relief, Prince Kung accepted the bargain.

And so it was that the Russians legitimized their ambitions on the Amur and acquired, signed, and sealed a strategic coastal area reaching southward to the Sea of Japan, including the site of Vladivostok.

Not being a people who leave matters to chance or treaties, the Russians had not been idle, waiting for Ignatiev to negotiate in Peking. Three years before this ingratiating young man had done Prince Kung the memorable favor, the ground had been laid in Siberia and the maritime region by an authentic empire builder whose later title attested to his accomplishments, General Count Nikolai Nikolayevich Muraviev-Amurski. This frontiersman-statesman had by guile and show of force established Russia illegally on the Amur and then bamboozled the Manchu frontier officials into a "treaty" authorizing Russian occupation, even before Ignatiev was on his way to Peking. And by the time the site of Vladivostok had been legally signed over in Peking, Muraviev had already begun building this bastion that confirmed Russia as a Pacific power.

Nearly forty years later, apprehensive over aggressive Japanese intent toward Manchuria, China formed in 1896 a secret defensive alliance with Russia. It followed from that collaborative relationship that Russia acquired rights to build and operate a railroad across northern Manchuria, a port, Dalny, and what was to become a major naval base, Port Arthur. Thus Russia moved, at China's expense, yet farther southward.

After the Bolsheviks came to power more than two decades later, Lenin righteously denounced past Russian behavior toward China as scandalous "spoilation." But, Dalny
and Port Arthur having been lost to Japan, he did not have
them to give back. Nor did he offer to return the Soviet
Far East, including Vladivostok.

Hence in a 1924 treaty with Peking, Moscow consented
that the Chinese would not recognize, in effect, the Mon-
golian People's Republic. The Chinese position was not surprising, as the MPR had been created in Outer Mongolia,
claimed by Peking as part of China. The Soviet agreement
to the Chinese denial of recognition to the MPR was meaningless because it did not confirm, on Moscow's part, Chinese sovereignty over Outer Mongolia. The realities of the
situation remained unchanged. The MPR was ostensibly an
independent state, but it had been created by the Red Army
and Soviet political agents and was covertly controlled by
the Kremlin. It was the first specimen of that captive political organism—a Soviet satellite state.

The Bolsheviks' un-self-denying agreement on the MPR
is a gem of its kind. The liberators of the oppressed peoples
of the East obviously gave nothing in the compact, assumed
no responsibility, gained credit for liberality, and retained
all that they had—for the MPR remained, and still is, within
the Soviet orbit. The czarist Ignatiev was, by comparison,
an amateur.

It was for Stalin to show how really to exploit friends and
use people for influence. He decided that world revolution
in his time was a piece of romanticism and that those who
seriously pressed for it should be done away with, which

he did. He decided that socialism in one country, the Soviet Union, should be the Bolshevik goal and that all foreign Communist parties should dedicate themselves to the defense of the U.S.S.R. at whatever cost to themselves. This might be rationalized on the grounds that only through ensuring the survival and growth of the Soviet Union did they have any chance eventually of winning. This, of course, was not necessarily true.

In Asia the threat to the Soviet state was initially, in the Kremlin's eyes, the United States and Japan. As Lenin put it in 1920: "The practical task of Communist policy is to take advantage of this hostility [between the United States and Japan] and to incite one against the other. . . . We have already set Japan and America at loggerheads, to put it crudely, and have thereby gained an advantage."

Stating the strategy in broad general terms, Lenin laid down the rule: "We Communists must use one country against another."

To Stalin, fairly faithful disciple of Lenin, it was evident that Japan's expansionist ambitions on the mainland of Asia were the immediate menace and that before the Japanese and Americans clashed in an imperialist war, Japan would expand westward to the peril of the Soviet Union. The policy decision was simple. Since the United States could not be depended upon to check westward Japanese aggression, use China against Japan. Find the strongest indigenous element in China and induce it to engage and contain the aggression. That element was the Kuomintang. The role of the weak, infant Chinese communist movement was to collaborate with the national bourgeois party and to press for national unity and resistance to foreign encroachments. Stalin's China policy was one of the main issues in dispute between him and Trotsky, who urged all-out revolution by the Chinese party. Stalin's policy resulted in the decimation of the Communists when Chiang Kai-shek, who had ardently cooperated with his Soviet advisers, turned on the Chinese Communists in 1927 and caused great numbers of them to be liquidated. Mao, absenting himself from collaboration with the Kuomintang, was one of those who escaped Chiang's executioners.

He soon drew Stalin's wrath for basing himself in the countryside on peasant support. He ignored Comintern orders to concentrate on the small urban proletariat. Moscow thereupon denounced him as a deviationist. Mao continued to go his own way.

But he did not disavow Moscow. The differences with the Kremlin were tactical, not over the basic body of doctrine. It was therefore not surprising that, when Chiang's punitive campaigns against him made his position in Central China untenable, the Long March took Mao and his troops to Northwest China, closer to the Soviet border.

By then, 1935, Stalin's united-front policy was in force. The German and Japanese threats had matured. And Stalin's Chinese converts dutifully recited the united-front catechisms. They even negotiated the release of Chiang, when the generalissimo had been fortuitously captured by disaffected warlord troops, on the condition that he form a united front in resistance to the Japanese.

By 1937 the Japanese had begun their full-scale invasion of China. This evoked a Sino-Soviet treaty, including a clause that bound the Russians, as well as the Chinese, "to refrain from taking any action or entering into any agreement which may be used by the aggressor or aggressors to the disadvantage of the Party subjected to aggression." Soviet supplies, loans, and a "volunteer" air unit went to Chiang, not to the Communists.

As Japan wasted its strength on the vast expanse of China, which offered a low-grade but draining resistance, the Nazis poised themselves to strike in Europe. To deflect the Germans, Molotov signed in 1939 a nonaggression pact with von Ribbentrop which released Hitler a week later to begin World War II. Thanks to the Kremlin, Hitler was able to say: "For the first time in history we have to fight only on one front." And when Hitler began to turn his attention to the U.S.S.R. in 1941, the Kremlin concluded a nonaggression pact with Matsuoka, whom Stalin embraced as a "fellow Asiatic." The agreement released Japan to go adventuring southward, away from the U.S.S.R., against the United States. And it meant that when the Germans attacked him, Stalin had to fight on only one front.

The news of Pearl Harbor must have been welcome tidings to the Kremlin. Lenin's prophetic policy had been fulfilled. Japan and the United States had turned "their knives against each other." The Kremlin could relax in Asia—until the time came to be in on the kill of Japan. The colonial war of the Japanese against the Chinese had been turned into an imperialist war between Japan and the United States.

With Japan an American problem and its expulsion from China a growing likelihood, the fancies of Chiang, Mao, and Stalin turned to thoughts of—after the Japanese, what in

China?

Chiang was determined to reoccupy all of China and share with no one his rule over the entire country. He was more than the legitimate chief of the Chinese state. He had been ordained by Roosevelt as one of the Big Four, in company with Churchill and Stalin. Postwar China was to be his.

Mao did not endorse this vision. And the Chinese Communists, who were growing in strength during the war as the Nationalists were being diminished, were rapidly becoming powerful enough to challenge Chiang's intentions.

They were willing to discuss a coalition government with the Kuomintang. But, remembering Chiang's interpretation of a coalition from their near extermination in the comradely collaboration of 1927, they demanded so strong a position in a coalition that Chiang could only reject their proposals. They expected this and used the negotiations to play for time as they improved their strategic relationship with the Nationalists. For, increasingly, they believed that with the Japanese defeat by the Americans, the imperialist war should be turned into a civil war, a war of liberation—liberation of China by themselves from everyone else.

Stalin had his own ideas for the future of China. He and Molotov, during the period 1943–45, professed to various American dignitaries their disinterest in and even contempt of their Chinese comrades—"margarine Communists"—and a desire to see China unified. Chiang Kai-shek, they confided, was the only one to unify China, and the United States should support him in that endeavor.

Dedijer tells us in his biography of Tito that Stalin in 1948 revealed to a Yugoslav delegation that the Kremlin had told the Chinese Communists not to resort to civil war because they could not win, and that therefore they should seek accommodation with and join the Nationalist government and disband their army. According to Dedijer, Stalin admitted that, in disregarding Soviet injunctions, the Chinese comrades had proved themselves right and the Kremlin wrong.

The Chinese would readily agree that in this respect, at least, Stalin was mistaken. They have gone further than that. Liu Shao-chi has spoken of the Kremlin's "erroneous tendencies" throughout the Chinese revolutionary struggle from 1921 to 1949.

Why was Stalin mistaken? Did he really calculate that the Chinese Communists could not make the grade? Possibly he did. But if so, he was either incredibly poorly served by or willfully disregardful of his intelligence service. And if he thought that the best thing for the Chinese comrades was to come to terms with Chiang and disarm, why did he urge the Americans to back Chiang? Such support, he must surely have anticipated, would stiffen Nationalist demands which, if yielded to, would reduce the Communists, if not to fugitives, certainly to subordination. This would be selling his Chinese retainers down the Yangtze, treating them worse than he had in the 1920s.

Was Stalin mistaken or was he deceitful? It is difficult to believe that he was unaware that his proposals were unworkable. The Chinese Communists were too powerful, too ambitious, and too close to their big chance to sacrifice themselves at his behest. The days of self-immolation were gone when the Chinese party had been a captive creature, as other foreign Communist parties still were. It is therefore implausible that Stalin, as a graduate revolutionary, did not foresee the near inevitability of civil war and at least the possibility of a communist victory in it.

If so, what was Stalin trying to do in his devious way? In searching for his motivation, the first place to look is at his obsession with the security and power of the Soviet state.

With the defeat of Japan, what would be the principal power issue for the Kremlin in East Asia? It would be the advance of American power westward into Japan, Korea, and China, into proximity with the U.S.S.R. Stalin would counter this, as he did, by occupying southern Sakhalin, the Kuriles, northern Korea, and Manchuria, thereby forestalling American contact with the hypersensitive Soviet frontier. Such insulation was a primitive necessity, but not enough to satisfy the Russian neurosis over security.

The Americans would still be uncomfortably close and powerful. They must therefore be kept busy, diverted from the Soviet Union. And what could be more distracting for them than undertaking to unify China under Stalin's old protégé Chiang Kai-shek? So Stalin's plea to American statesmen that their government back the Nationalists was sincere, as sincere as the exhortations of a Charles Addams character urging an innocent to explore a swamp at midnight.

All this was not unrelated to Stalin's ruminations about the future of Europe. His interest in exploiting the more inviting postwar possibilities in Europe exceeded his attraction to Asia. Consequently it would be helpful to him if the United States became preoccupied with Asia.

Stalin may not have foreseen open Chinese defiance of and hostility to the Kremlin in the 1960s. But his instincts were correct. He did not trust—more precisely, find acceptable—any party that was not Stalinized, that was not penetrated by his own men, into which he could not immediately reach to punish or purge.

The Chinese party could hardly have been found acceptable by Stalin. Mao was surrounded by people loyal to Mao, first and last, from his Politburo, through the police apparatus, to the Chinese Red Army. And Mao was not servile. He was headstrong. If he had defied the Kremlin and stubbornly gone his own way when he was weak, how much more rambunctious he was likely to become at the war's end, with his own armies and the possibility of a revolutionary triumph in sight.

Stalin was one of the unsilliest statesmen of history. He was totally uninterested in the triumph of communism in China simply to liberate the Chinese proletariat and peasantry. A communist revolution and victory not controlled by the Kremlin was, for him, disorderly adventurism. It was dangerous to Soviet interests and should be prevented.

Therefore the Chinese party had first to be Stalinized. After that, revolution could be considered, planned, and executed, as convenient and useful to the Soviet Union.

To Stalinize the Chinese party meant, initially, to reduce it in power, reduce it to dependance on the U.S.S.R. so that the Kremlin could penetrate the party, police, and army. Ideally, the Chinese communist military forces should be disbanded and the party weakened through submission to a coalition with the Nationalists. But if Mao refused to do this and plunged ahead into civil war, then the conflict should be so contrived as to force the Communists sooner or later into deep reliance upon Moscow.

Obviously, the chastisement and humbling of the Chinese Communists was neither a suitable nor a convenient undertaking for the Soviet Union. It was in the bolshevik tradition that someone else should see to it that the punishment was administered. Who better than the Americans?

If they would back the ineffectual Nationalists in their try at unifying China against the military challenge of the Communists, three Soviet ends would be served. The United States would be distracted from Europe into an entanglement in China. Mao would be forced into supplication to the U.S.S.R. and thereby made vulnerable to Kremlin control. And in the process, the Chinese Communists and the Americans would come so to abominate one another that, should the revolution succeed, relations between the two would be satisfactorily envenomed for years to come. A Red China would take Japan's place as the principal adversary of the United States in Asia. The two would be set at loggerheads.

This scheme turned out to be but a partial success. Its greatest failure was the inability of the Kremlin to penetrate and capture the Chinese party and state apparatus. By the late 1950s and early 1960s, when the Russians had begun to be alarmed by the growth of Chinese power and ambition, no one could have wished more than Khrushchev that Chiang, rather than Mao, was ruling China.

Nor, by then, could anyone have much more reason than the American Joint Chiefs of Staff to wish that the nuclearly sophisticated Kremlin, rather than the adventuristic Mao Dynasty, controlled China.

But that was not and is not the case. China is ruled by the Chinese Politburo. And it is in an ugly, vindictive mood, even though it may come to dissemble it.

The Chinese want their vengeance on the Russians for all that has passed. More particularly, they want it for Moscow's loot of Manchuria at the close of World War II, and for Khrushchev's reduction of Soviet aid and withdrawal of technical advisers, both essential to China's economic development. They have a score to settle because of the Kremlin's selfish great-power policy of coexistence with the imperialists, its suspiciously status-quo fudging on revolutionary militancy, and its craven refusal in the late fifties and early sixties to unleash on the United States a nuclear war of mutual obliteration, out of which enough millions of Chinese would have survived to make and dominate a classless world, with nothing to lose but its radioactivity.

The possibility of a *détente* between the Soviet bloc and the West worries Peking. That would truly isolate China and defer its attainment of a great-power position by decades if not indefinitely.

There are two courses by which Peking might overcome this isolation. One would be a *détente* with the West, out of which China would try to extract capital and technical aid. Even with Western Europe alone, or with Japan, this would be difficult for Peking, involving an ideological loss of face. But it is not impossible.

The alternative would be a *détente* with Moscow. The Kremlin, however, is so suspicious of Peking's pretensions and potential that Moscow's price for renewed large-scale aid would be exceedingly high—hardly less than the abdication of Mao and the acceptance of Soviet primacy. Such a bargain could hardly appeal to the Mao Dynasty.

Otherwise Peking is on its own, essentially alone, with a gnawing dilemma—the ratio of limited natural resources and geometrically growing population. The ratio has been widening. The demands of population increase, notwithstanding a birth-control campaign, hobble economic development and sap national power.

In its frustration, Peking seeks to undermine Moscow by resorting to racial appeals to Africa, the rest of Asia, and Latin America. This is, of course, Marxist heresy. But never mind, so long as it makes the Kremlin squirm.

Racism, however, will not solve China's crucial economic problems, even if it wins Peking the support of the underdeveloped peoples of the world. It would be the poor leading the poor. And in that union, in the modern world, there is not likely to be much strength.

In desperation Peking may attempt to invade some of its southern neighbors to liberate and exploit them. But this would not make up for the enormous deficiencies in China, at least not for a generation, if by then. As for Chinese irredentism and envy of Soviet land, the Russians are surely not going to be obliging.

So long as it is politically cohesive, China is a mighty military power on the defensive. Against its nonnuclear continental neighbors it is superior on the offensive. But its offensive capabilities against a major nuclear power are limited, if the defender is willing to use nuclear weapons to countervail the Chinese human sea. The Russians would have no compunctions about so reacting. Nor would they feel squeamish about a preemptive nuclear strike at a growing nuclear capability.

As an underdeveloped country confronted by a staggering demographic versus resources dilemma and driven by an irrational ideology, China is an extreme example of those poor nations that, no matter how they seem to progress, are being steadily outdistanced by the rich, advanced states. The advanced powers are growing in strength in relation to the poor as the problems of the poor are multiplying. None can understand better than the Chinese that "to him that hath shall be given, and from him that hath not shall be taken away." China hath not.

Europa and the Bull in the China Shop

One of the more curious phenomena of the years following World War II was the American astigmatism regarding nationalism.

In this vision, international organizations loomed large and luminous. The United Nations was seen in magnified dimensions and in deep perspective, towering in the distance as the magistrate of a world ordered by justice and law.

A plaid of alliances and international regional organizations—the North Atlantic Treaty Organization, the Southeast Asia Treaty Organization, the Organization of American States, and others—appeared more definitively than many of the nations composing them. And in the middle distance, the multinational blur of Western Europe seemed to be merging into shimmering focus as a united Europe.

Nationality was perceived, to be sure, in bright hues as the bewildering procession of new states entered the world scene. The eye took this in as a seemly and exotic sight.

Bulking close up and occupying most of the field of view was the Soviet Union, distinguished less as a nation than as the dominant part of an international bloc in which all nationality but the Russian had been crushed, extinguished.

What the retina did not register was the resurgence of nationalism in the Soviet Empire and in Western Europe. The Tito defection of 1948 was viewed as a surprising freak, and scarcely more than that. It was not generally seen as revelatory of nationalism alive within the monolith. Not until the late 1950s could one suggest without loss of respectability that self-assertive nationalism might exist in, for example, Communist China. Earlier in the decade, to raise such a thought was sufficient to excite a formal charge questioning a man's loyalty to the United States.

Recognition of the force of nationalism in Western Europe was even more tardy. As late as 1962 the Kennedy administration, leading the public, apparently saw the European idea as rampant and nationalism as an irritating but nonetheless secondary force. Consequently the assertion of French nationalism in de Gaulle's 1963 blackball of Britain from the Common Market club came as a staggering shock.

The changes that have been taking place in Europe, and will continue to, are the product of mainly four interacting impulses: the complex of internal forces at work within Western Europe, the growing restiveness in the Eastern European states under Soviet paramountcy, the zigzag of the Kremlin to the right, and the American commitment to and pressure on Western Europe.

The unification of Europe is not of course a new theme. Before Jean Monnet, there was Julius Caesar. The Roman did not boggle at including in his united Europe, as did Charles de Gaulle, the "insular, maritime" English with their "very marked and original customs and traditions." But then, they had not applied for membership; he applied it to them with his legions.

Historically, unification in Europe, whether partial as with Charlemagne, national as with Bismarck and Garibaldi, or extensive as with Napoleon, Hitler, and Stalin, has been achieved by force, applied and implied. Even the sensible Swiss underwent a civil war to reestablish unity.

As Stalin's Red Army imposed unity on Eastern Europe, the American and allied forces released the spirit of nationalism and diversity in Western Europe. American armed forces stayed on after the war and American influence continued predominant. This influence derived from military and economic commitments to Europe.

The postwar military commitment, formalized in NATO, guaranteed the defenseless Western Europeans the prerequisite for recovery—protection during their period of postwar convalescence. They were able then to concentrate on rehabilitation without due external distraction.

But the American military presence was not enough. An economic transfusion was essential. Hence the Marshall Plan. American aid interacted with the skills, the vitality, the genius, and the will of the Western Europeans to renew the countries from which American civilization first came. As this was happening, Western Europe was being freed, forcibly or somewhat less reluctantly, from what had become the dream and the throes of its colonial empires.

Thus reinvigorated and released, these old and gifted lands came to be essentially on their own, discovering a new and stimulating existence within themselves. This was true notwithstanding *ancien régime* bewilderment and grumbling. By the early sixties most Europeans were better off than they had ever been, as the vacation coasts of Spain and Italy attested.

This resurgence, and more, of well-being and confidence through most of Western Europe did not make its peoples draw significantly closer together as Europeans. Because they visited one another's countries in greater numbers than they had ever done before did not of itself make them continental-minded, except as members of the Volkswagen-Vespa international.

Getting to know one another better did not create a popular demand for Western European unity. Travel may broaden the outlook, but often only in the sense that it widens the range of prejudices. Because many Americans travel abroad does not incline them to recommend yielding one jot of national sovereignty to a common lot with the lands that they have visited.

Yet undeniably there has developed since 1949 some feeling of Europeanism. First, in negative terms, it was a revulsion against the ruinous folly of Europe's civil wars. It was also a feeling that another intra-European war would probably so incite the superpowers that they would usurp the conflict, collapsing the skies on all concerned. In positive terms it was an understanding that they, the people of the western half of this prodigious little continent, a peninsula on Asia, must somehow learn to live in mutual tolerance, if not unity.

Then, too, fear of the lowering Soviet Empire, to the extent that it was felt, tended to press many Western Europeans together. With others it was, by the 1960s, annoyance over American mothering and nagging, even the mere presence of American supremacy—probably the most effective contributions that we have made to Western European solidarity.

There were the European proponents of unity, proclaiming that in the logic of history the nations of that continent must advance toward integration. De Gaulle was, of course, such an advocate with his partially revealed formula for unity. There was also the Monnet school, the Spaak, the Hallstein, and others. As de Gaulle suggested in July, 1963, there were quite a number of fathers of Europe—at least, so far as went the gleam in the eye.

Quieter, almost inaudible but perhaps more influential, were those industrialists, bankers, and others who saw economic advantage in and even the necessity of a coalescence closer than that of the Common Market, an integrated Western Europe. For them unity was not something sought out of fear, irritation, a sense of history, or political ambition. It was out of a desire for profit and an orderly economic environment. These were and still are strong compulsions toward unity.

A variety of counterforces worked against or impeded the development of unity in Western Europe. There was the very vagueness of the concept of unity. Conflict exists over where a united Europe should begin—across the Channel, over the Pyrenees: where? And where would its eastern boundaries lie?

If fixed at the Elbe, what of the Germans beyond this Stygian stream? And if the political line of the Elbe is crossed, would unification proceed by the logic of geography to the Urals or by political reasoning to Vladivostok and to the Bering Strait, with Alaska as Europe's near neighbor?

What was meant by unity—Monnet's eventual United States of Europe, de Gaulle's confederation of fatherlands, or simply a customs union? There was no general agreement on what should be the goal.

Leaving this area of vagueness and indecision, there is no need to dwell upon the obvious, upon the mundane impediments to unity. None were insuperable, even though together they added up to a serious obstacle. They were, in sum, differing cultural heritages and outlooks.

What was and is crucial is the issue of sovereignty. Up to a point it can be yielded, peeled off like an artichoke. But not very far before the heart is exposed. The Common Market got close to the sensitive center when it peeled only to farm-product prices, which is still a long way from which European is to be empowered to pull the nuclear trigger.

The price of wheat or fruit or chickens involves the farm vote—and so politicians—and frequently laws governing subsidies and tariffs, and, because of import competition, often foreign affairs. The making, changing, and enforcement of laws are attributes of sovereignty. As Common Market negotiations came close to these issues of sovereignty they encountered mounting difficulty.

To most of us, a unified Europe means a merging, more or less, of the various national sovereignties making up the union. Most of us do not think of a confederation or customs union in which each state retains its governing powers.

But the merging of sovereignties is an all or nothing matter. To merge any significant part of sovereignty is to affect most other functions of sovereignty, leading either to total assimilation or, more likely, the aborting of an imperfect union.

Consider the example of military unification, which has been recommended as the most effective course to a united Western Europe. This integration goes beyond an alliance such as NATO, for in an alliance each sovereign government retains ultimate control over the units it contributes to a combined command. It also has a voice in the substantive decisions of that headquarters, if only to withdraw its commitment. We are not talking about committee control, as in an alliance, but amalgamation with decisions flowing from a single sovereign authority.

Assume the simplest situation: the six of the Common Market. Their population ratio in 1963 was roughly this, in millions: Germany 58, Italy 52, France 47, Netherlands 12, Belgium 10, Luxembourg 0.4. Shall a German, chosen from the most populous element, be empowered to commit Italians or Belgians to his personal reaction to a nuclear crisis? Or should it be a "directorate," or someone chosen by weighted voting or by a conventional kind of compromise, say a Spaak from a "little country" who, in an emergency, would cast the die for the French as well as the Germans?

In sum, which one man would be sovereign in Western Europe? For in the instantaneous nuclear age—hot lines or not, nonaggression pacts or mounting tensions—we are back to the condition in which the lives of multitudes rest, not in the palm of one man's hand but on his trigger finger.

The United States would not yield this life and death power to a foreigner. Would France or Germany voluntarily do so even though the foreigner were also Western European? Maybe. But if so, only with profound reluctance.

Unity through military merging raises many problems in addition to that of ultimate command. A series of sovereign rights in each country would have to be relinquished in favor of a unitary organism, even in a federal system.

Differing laws of conscription, or lack of conscription, must be reconciled. Pay scales, equipment, and amenities must be equalized. All these affect finances and therefore taxation. Are the Italians thus to make the second largest manpower contribution and, according to their gross national product, provide the lowest per capita financial support?

Because of language differences, it hardly seems practicable that integration of forces begin with the squad. Where, then, should merging begin—regiment, division, corps, or army? What about procurement and supply services? Should they be organized on a national pattern or should they be integrated?

Or perhaps the business of soldiering might be divided up as it was when Britain ruled a multiracial, multilingual India. The Sikhs and Rajputs, for example, were regarded as martial peoples and so were trained as front-line troops. The Madrasis, looked upon as less pugnacious, were generally assigned noncombat functions. There would be little doubt that the Germans, at least, would qualify for the martial role. But who of the rest, even if eminently qualified, would cheerfully and publicly accept the rational, actuarially sounder status of Europe's Madrasis?

Military integration is perhaps the most rugged of the voluntary routes to unification, for military functions and responsibilities quickly raise life, death, and money issues for the citizens and the state. They go to the nub of sovereignty and make abandonment of it for something new and untried seem onerous and chancey. And those who have vested interests in the perpetuation of the individual nation states—most politicians, professional soldiers, and bureaucrats—are naturally alert to the risks of unification.

As of 1964, none of the forces that might unify Western Europe were dominating the scene. There was no internal or external power able and willing to compel integration in the traditional manner. Nor was the vision of unity magnetic and captivating enough to draw the Western Europeans into spontaneous unification. And finally, the pressure of an external menace was not sufficiently felt to push the nations of Western Europe into amalgamation.

Two events dramatized this situation. One was de Gaulle's rejection in January, 1963, of British entry into the Common Market. Prior to this there was a widespread feeling that the movement for unity was advancing steadily toward completion and that Britain would be a part of the new union. Actually, the six of the Common Market had not gone far; they had not come to any issue of vital national economic concern such as basic agricultural policy. The question of British membership braked the momentum of unification before it ran into the obdurate problems close to the core of national sovereignty.

The second event was the American-Soviet crisis in October, 1962, over the Kremlin's placement of "offensive" missiles on Cuba. The Kennedy administration chose to challenge only the threat of these medium-range missiles, not the Soviet military presence in Cuba. Although Khrushchev was thus allowed to save some face when he retreated on this limited front, it was clear to all that an apparent American willingness to proceed to nuclear war had forced the Soviet Union to back down.

To the Western Europeans, the outcome of the Cuban crisis—a dry run on a nuclear showdown between the superpowers—confirmed two hitherto vaguely held assumptions. One was that, when exercised with a display of resolution, the American deterrent was persuasive to the Russians. Therefore, so long as the United States remained powerful and committed to the defense of Western Europe, there was no great danger of Soviet invasion. The pressure toward unity, caused by the menace from the East, consequently declined.

Secondly, Cuba brought home to the Western Europeans that, without their having any voice in the matter, they could nevertheless suddenly be placed in mortal peril by a confrontation between the nuclear giants over a Caribbean island, or some other unlikely spot, in which the average Frenchman, German, or Italian and his government had not the slightest interest. Consequently the Cuban object lesson also strengthened in some, conspicuously de Gaulle, the belief that Western Europe should develop its own nuclear power in an effort to acquire control of its own destiny. With many more it reinforced the inclination to get out from between, out of the dangerous, tiresome crunch of the superpowers—and into neutralism.

Most Western Europeans were in an unheroic frame of mind. After having been mauled through two great wars, their instincts were pacific. Behind a scarcely seen American nuclear shield, they wanted to go each about his own business. After having ourselves lived for nearly a hundred years behind the shield of British naval power, we Americans should be able to appreciate this attitude. So Western Europe was also isolationist, as isolationist as anyone between two vastly more potent forces dares or can contrive to be.

Neutralist, pacific, isolationist, and also vital—the enormous creative drive of the Western Europeans found expression in materialism. The creation and enjoyment of things became a dominating end in life. And as the productivity of these extraordinary people grows, they approach the suffocation of abundance, of a productive capacity exceeding the demands of their existing markets.

Where more logically do they turn for new markets than to Eastern Europe? Most of the countries across the Curtain have complementary economies; most suffer from a shortage of manufactured products—and they are neighbors. The main obstacle in the way of a West-East common market of course, is political.

By 1963 there seemed to be some signs of a slow change getting under way. Nationalism was coming alive in the Soviet satellites. The most conspicuous case was the Rumanian defiance of the Comecon (the communist common market). Khrushchev's Comecon scheme was for the international division of labor. Rumania was designated as one of the raw-material producers, exchanging these commodities for manufactured goods from those nations appointed by Moscow to make the finished products for the whole of the Comecon.

But Rumanian national pride did not accept a rustic destiny. It demanded the conventional status symbol of national respectability—a steel mill. Rumania had surplus petroleum to trade. So flouting the Comecon dispensation and scorning shoddy Eastern European machinery, the Rumanians proceeded to buy a Western European plant, paying with oil. At the same time, Bucharest blackmailed Moscow on the issue of supporting the Russians against the Chinese, extracting not only Soviet acceptance of Rumania's extramural dealings but also aid in the building of Rumanian heavy industry.

Yugoslavia is a more advanced example of a communist-ruled state's going its own nationalistic way, coexisting and trading with the East and the West. It may be a prototype of the Eastern European countries a decade or two hence. This is not to say that the satellites will break abruptly as Tito did with Stalin, creating a Marxist scandal for all the world to see.

It seems more likely, if the Kremlin continues the flexible course which it pursued in the early sixties, that its Eastern European protectorates will inconspicuously develop into something resembling dominion status. That is to say, they will in varying degrees assert increasing political and economic independence of Moscow without rupturing relations or withdrawing from the communist commonwealth. And interacting with this growing sense of separate identity in each nation will probably be a broadening of economic relations with Western Europe, a discovery and expansion of many interests in common.

East Germany, however, is not a part of this picture. It is a rump state with no real political personality of its own. Its people look west to the real Germany from which they were cut off and with which they want to be reunited. The regime is reminiscent of those native colonial administrations detested by their own people and dependent upon the imperial power. It is therefore more bolshevik than the Kremlin and will continue to lag in political development behind the rest of Eastern Europe.

Because the German Democratic Republic is a prime strategic buffer for the U.S.S.R., the Kremlin might well be anxious were this Marxist margravate to show the same restiveness that has been displayed elsewhere in the Soviet sphere. Consequently Russian inclinations to maintain a firm control, together with Ulbrichtian servility to Moscow, will probably combine to make East Germany something of an anachronism in the socialist camp a decade hence.

It is difficult to see how the people of this miserable pseudo-state can come to have an authentic political existence except in reunion with the true Germany. And that can probably come about only as a result of a fundamental change in West-East relations: one that quiets Russian neuroses (and French anxieties) about Germans, or a reorientation of West Germany away from the Atlantic Alliance and into collaboration with the East.

If, through the sixties and beyond, the Kremlin continues with the peaceful-coexistence line, it will be because objective conditions, as the Communists say, indicate such a policy. Were the Soviet Union to acquire a decisive power superiority over the United States, the objective conditions would differ. Under such conditions, another line, assumably arbitrary, would be adopted. To discuss such an eventuality would open a floodgate of speculation. For the derivatives of disaster are a whole new field of inquiry.

Hence for present intelligibility we continue on the assumption that the U.S.S.R. will not be in a military position to dictate to the rest of the world. In such a situation, a return to a hard line by the Kremlin would be a reversion to the rigidities and tyrannies of Stalinism. This in turn would incite embarrassing defections by Russia's Eastern European auxiliaries. An increasing isolation of the Soviet Union would probably ensue, leaving it and the United States, the two superpowers, in lonely confrontation across the Arctic, watching their respective European allies quietly depolarizing into closer association with one another.

Should, however, the Kremlin continue with its policy of the early sixties—a looser rein on its Eastern European dependencies and peaceful coexistence with the capitalist West —it stands to gain certain advantages. Some will be in Eastern Europe, others in Western Europe.

If the Kremlin rolls with the punch of nationalism, revisionism, and right deviations in Eastern Europe, it may be able to hold the bloc together longer than it otherwise could. Thus Stalin's empire might develop ultimately into a socialist commonwealth, with allegiance not to the first secretary of the Soviet Central Committee but to broadly interpreted principles of Marxism-Leninism.

This elastic strategy has already permitted the Kremlin to imply that an impenitent, suspicious Tito was a prodigal son welcomed back in the Marxist-Leninist family notwithstanding his dissolute carryings on with the imperialists.

But a common ideology, however adhesive, will not be binding enough over the long run—hence the Comecon, the plan for international socialist division of labor, a system of economic interdependence. With each nation of the Soviet sphere allotted a specialized production role according to its resources, plant, and manpower capabilities, the system was to function on the principle of mass production, with the Soviet Union and satellites as a huge unified market. Thus the Kremlin would create a network of clients economically tied to the U.S.S.R. and to one another.

The plan, of course, has not worked out as plotted. The main reason that it has not has been nationalism: particularist economic ambitions and the desire of most countries to be as self-sufficient as possible. Nevertheless the Comecon has served the Kremlin better than no plan at all, even though not much better.

Ideological permissiveness was added by the Kremlin to peaceful coexistence to make a sauce to tempt Western Europe. Peaceful coexistence was the body for the old popular-front mix, and Kremlin acceptance of right deviations in the various Communist parties of Western Europe provided the nationalist flavoring.

Italy is an example. By 1963 the Kremlin had pretty well persuaded the Italians that the Soviet Union had abandoned aggression and wanted no more than to compete peacefully with the West. The fear of being overrun by Tartar hordes from the East had subsided. The Christian Democrats opened to the left, the Italian Communists opened to the right, and Pope John's encyclicals were taken as license to fellow-travel with the Communists. Unless the parties of the center regain the confidence of the people, Italian politics will probably polarize to the left and to the right. And the attraction which the well-organized Communists will exert is likely to grow if they continue to Italianize their policy.

In the rest of Western Europe the Communists enjoyed less marked success except in France, where the party regained much of the respectability that it had lost because of the barbaric Soviet suppression of the Hungarian uprising. This was due in no small measure to the socialist left's cozying up to the Communists out of opportunism and the fuzziness characteristic of many European intellectuals. If the party can nationalize itself further and ingratiate itself with the public, it may come to do as well as its Italian comrades.

In Germany it was another matter. There were few illusions about domestic communism in the Federal Republic. East Germany was a gruesome exhibition of applied bolshevism lying there in front of West German eyes.

If in Western Europe the Kremlin holds to the strategy of peaceful coexistence and indulgence of national communism, the movement may gain in both adherents and influence. The party might eventually even come to power in one or several countries. But should this occur, it is not certain that the new communist regimes would be subservient to Moscow.

For in accepting national communism, most conspicuously in the case of Tito's Yugoslavia but also in the instance of Togliatti in Italy, the Kremlin has yielded to what Togliatti has called polycentrism. The concept of various centers of a common faith is perhaps better expressed in terms of the Orthodox Church. The trend of communism in the early sixties was in the direction of an autocephalous organization.

This all serves to present communism as an indulgent ecumenical movement. But what does it add up to for the Kremlin? It is a drift away from the small, hard-core principle of Lenin and Stalin, in disciplined obedience to the infallible Soviet center of power and authority. It may add to Soviet popularity, but does it add to Soviet power?

The ultimate risk to the Kremlin of such a process is that Khrushchev or his successor ends up as the Bolshevik Patriarch of Russia—and little more. But what is the Kremlin's alternative once the process has gone as far as it has? A fall-back to rigidity, fragmentation, and final isolation.

The American entanglement in Europe is strategic in origin. This has been so since the second decade of this century. It is a cardinal tenet of American strategy that Europe must not come under the domination of one nation because the resulting concentration of power would exceed ours and, sooner or later, probably challenge us.

The United States fought two great wars to stop this from happening. At the end of the second conflict an ally, the Soviet Union, had come to dominate one-half of Europe and clearly intended by one means or another to bring the remainder of the continent under its sway, if not prevented from doing so.

Washington diagnosed the danger correctly. It was two-fold. One was the military challenge of the Soviet Union. The other was the economic and political anemia of Western Europe, making it vulnerable to varied forms of Soviet indirect aggression. In reacting to the danger, the basic response of the Truman administration was brilliantly conceived and executed: (1) to meet the military challenge, an increase in American military strength and the creation of NATO; (2) to make possible the recovery of Western Europe, the Marshall Plan.

For the United States, the efforts to save Western Europe were really a function of the cold war. Western Europe was to Washington but one, albeit the most important, theater of conflict in a global struggle. It was a frustrating struggle because of its elusive form and because, for the West, it was essentially defensive, with no definition of what would constitute victory. It was against the grain of the American temperament, the impulse for a clear-cut win in any situation of conflict.

Most Western Europeans, however, did not share the militant, global view of the cold war. They tended to suspect that there could be no clear-cut victory, with Western Europe unscathed and the Russian bear shot between the eyes, skinned and stretched out before the hearth. Their horizon did not extend much beyond Europe, and the best that they expected was that the Soviet menace be contained and that in the meantime Western Europe recover and flourish.

American impatience with the inconclusive course of the cold war rose during the early 1950s. The Eisenhower administration proclaimed a policy of liberation of Eastern Europe and rumbled about the necessity of going to the brink of war. This alarmed the Western Europeans even though the more worldly wise recognized the thunder out of Foggy Bottom as the bombast of any new administration out to create a virile image on the cheap.

For when the test came in 1956 with the anguished uprising in Hungary, the brink to which Washington, with proper prudence, advanced was that of utter frustration. It was saved from going over the edge by the therapeutic hallucination of the United Nations, in which dilemmas can be deposited with the illusion that by referring a baffling problem to a Higher Entity it may be resolved; but if not, at least one's conscience (and image) are absolved of the guilt of inaction.

The second Eisenhower term was marked by a more sober posture toward the cold war. There was a return to the essentially defensive strategy of containment, with the implied hope that eventually the Soviet Empire would thus be forced to mend its ways. This policy was more in accord with the attitude of the European members of NATO. And it was more consonant with the North Atlantic Treaty, which provided for a defensive, not an offensive, alliance.

Meanwhile, as Western Europe was recovering, it became evident that one of the reasons for the success of the Marshall Plan was collaborative effort among the participating Europeans. Recognition of the benefits flowing from cooperation led to the creation in 1949 of a platonic Council of Europe and in 1952 of the Coal and Steel Community, a sanitized supercartel.

Also in 1952 a treaty was signed providing for a European Defense Community with integrated forces. The concept was sheer political hashish. As such, it stimulated visions in some: delusions that European nation states had begun to reenact the eighteenth-century drama of thirteen British colonies on the rim of the New World forming a more perfect union. The intoxication wore off in a couple of years. There was a reluctant return to consciousness of the real environment, one of pervasive nationalism.

But Washington's craving for a unified Western Europe was still strong. Looking for its new frontier after coming to office, the Kennedy administration discovered it in clearing out the slums, oligarchs, and jungles of Latin America —and in unifying Western Europe. The plan for the winning of the West in the Old World was called, in all simplicity, the grand design. It was an ingenuous if intellectually calisthenic concept of a united Western Europe in partnership with the United States.

The fiasco of the grand design, again because of nationalism, does not mean that Western Europe will not someday, eventually, be peacefully united. Reemphasizing what has been said, there are strong economic reasons for Western European unity. There are also strong reasons for partnership with the United States—but also with Eastern Europe. For over the long haul the politicoeconomic changes taking place in both halves of Europe may lead not simply to an integrated Western Europe but to a coalescence of all Europe.

This seemed to be what Khrushchev was aiming at in 1963. And if peaceful coexistence is maintained, the Kremlin's goal might not be more difficult to achieve than that of a policy aimed at causing one-half of Europe to unite, to turn its back against the other half of the continent, and to seek across the Atlantic partnership with the United States, subject to the advice and consent of the Senate.

In the competition between Washington's grand design and Moscow's peaceful coexistence, it was ironic that the United States, priding itself on its diversity and universal appeal, should have followed the more restricted policy. To be sure, Washington would have rejoiced at the overthrow of communist governments in the satellites, and Moscow was determined to bury, if it could, capitalist governments and institutions in Western Europe. The difference was that peaceful coexistence asked less of the Western Europeans and was seemingly more permissive to them than the grand design.

If American strategy is still based on the proposition that the domination of Europe by one power would critically imperil our security, it is fair to ask whether a policy of artificially forcing the pace of unification of even a part of Europe is consistent with such a strategy. It would seem that an acceptance of national diversity in the western half of the continent and its practical encouragement in the eastern portion are strategically sounder—and more workable because more in accord with the inclinations of the Europeans.

With its enormous and versatile nuclear capability, it is difficult to see why the United States needs a Western European contribution of the dimensions that we ask to deter Soviet attack. Likewise it is questionable that we need to maintain a force in being on the continent for this purpose.

Washington's preoccupation with the military aspects of the transatlantic relationship, its persistent exhortations to its NATO allies to increase their armed strength, its premature, unsolicited introduction of the tricky issue of nuclear armaments for the Germans, its multiloquent improvisation of a multilateral, multinational nuclear fleet, all these may have been militarily sound, but they were not psychologically sound. They irritated many Western Europeans without really accomplishing what Washington wanted.

American nuclear superiority is essential to the security of Western Europe. But in the sixties the cold war in Europe was not being fought on the basis of military considerations. Soviet cold-war aggression was less in crude military threats than in economic, political, and psychological ingratiation. It was an offensive in attraction, in magnetism.

There are reasons to think that it will not work, principally because of the basic defects of the Soviet system. But it is certainly a far shrewder and more subtle policy than attempts at intimidation. And it is one in which Washington has shown no genius in countering.

We are concerned with what our role of leadership in Europe should be. That is not the issue for us. Our first problem with Europe is to understand it, to catch up with what has been going on across the Atlantic. Then we can consider whether indeed we have a leadership role—or a more relaxed one as collaborator.

Disgraceful and Ruinous Mutability?

*A*merica . . . finds that she is held in no respect by her friends; that she is the derision of her enemies; and that she is a prey to every nation which has an interest in speculating on her fluctuating councils and embarrassed affairs."

These are not the words of the 1964 Republican candidate for the presidency. These are the words of Publius (probably James Madison rather than Alexander Hamilton), writing in 1778.

The humiliations suffered by the country were "the mischievous effects of a mutable government," of a frequent turnover in personnel and policies. "These causes together," predicted Hamilton in a later number of the *Federalist Papers*, "could not fail to occasion a disgraceful and ruinous mutability in the administration of the government."

A century and three-quarters later, discontinuity and amateurism in the administration of our public affairs plague the Federal executive. The general public is so inured to administrative erraticism that it hardly seems to notice it.

Successive waves of new functionaries revel in their chance to shape events with new schemes. The tired old bureaucrats are resigned to discouragement. And a few senators worry about executive turnover.

Before looking more closely at the contemporary Federal executive scene, it may be illuminating to scan three foreign institutions with a tradition of professionalism and continuity in service.

The Confucian literati, the English public school, and the Communist party of the Soviet Union belong to civilizations about as unlike as can be imagined. And yet these institutions are significantly alike in a number of respects.

Each in its own completely different way trained the youth who were to become the administrators of great empires. Each inculcated its dogma (Confucianist or Communist) or a cultural outlook (in the case of the public school), indoctrinating the future managers of empire with a common interpretation of the destiny of the empire, the function of government, and the disciplined role of the individual official and his proper relations with others in the hierarchy of power.

The youths who underwent this rigorous training were not a random group; nor were they a cross section of the respective societies. Those who studied under the Confucian literati were for the most part sons of men who had sufficient means to hire tutors and maintain the lad while he pursued his studies of the classics.

So it also was with the public school, a stronghold of the aristocracy and of the new upper middle class. Nor is the party open to all comers. It, too, has its criteria, occult rather than class—although the offspring of the proletarian peerage now constitute a snob group.

Thus they were select elements trained to administer the three empires. They were select groups drilled to patterns of power responsibility and to communicating with one another, each in its own vocabulary, in a common language in which all of the basic criteria for judgments and action were understood and agreed upon.

Not all who underwent this indoctrination made the grade. Those who did passed into the mandarinate of Imperial China, the establishment in Britain, and the party-government apparatus in the Soviet Union.

The mandarinate, the establishment, and the apparatus were composed almost exclusively of officials who had undergone this selective preparation. Government was by professionals. It was a lifetime career. Only rarely would an amateur, someone unconditioned for the management of public affairs, make his way, through talent or favor, into the governing group.

The management of public affairs was looked upon in the three civilizations as of the highest importance. The mandarinate, the establishment, and the apparatus were, therefore, accorded honored status. They were elite groups, and those who belonged to them enjoyed special privileges. These benefits were, naturally, an incentive to compete for a place in official life and to remain in it, for there was no more attractive career.

Because of the systematic indoctrination and the professional character of those engaged in administering the three empires, there tended to be an economy of effort in the discharge of official duties. Philosophical points of view and basic assumptions about the state, the individual, the world, and national goals were established and accepted. Consequently discussion and decision ordinarily concentrated on the subject at issue.

Sometimes, of course, the basic assumptions turned out to be wrong and all the operational policy flowing therefrom to be damaging or downright disastrous, as witness the mandarinate's reaction to the impact of the West and the communist apparatus's policy on agriculture. This defect, however, is not peculiar to a professionalized ruling group. It is only that when an error is made, it is more systematically perpetrated than in a government in which all philosophical premises and basic assumptions are under recurrent, rambling exploration and subject to individualistic interpretations and applications at all levels of the bureaucracy.

The career composition of mandarinate, establishment, and apparatus brought continuity to the administration of empire. There was no procession of rotating amateurs undergoing in-job training. The inherent weakness in such secure tenure and continuity of personnel lies in a tendency toward stagnation rather than erraticism and caprice.

The mandarinate, the establishment, and the apparatus have not been, of course, immune to the historical forces of corruption and decay. The mandarinate crumbled with the decomposition of the classic Chinese Empire—after two thousand years of administering vast domains. The establishment, after a century (although some will say much longer) of dominance, has markedly declined. If it re-forms its structure and widens its base, it may regain vitality. The apparatus is new on the scene, its endurance and that of the empire it manages yet to be proved.

It is a long way from mandarinate, establishment, and apparatus to our national-policy machinery, the system by which we manage our national affairs.

The succession of studies and investigations of the federal government in recent years is symptomatic of the general anxiety over the way we are handling our governmental activities. Perhaps the most authoritative, because the most informed and exhaustive, is the report of the Senate subcommittee on national policy machinery. On the basis of two years of work and some eighteen hundred pages of hearings and documentary material, the chairman, Senator Henry M. Jackson, announced in November, 1961, that "the heart problem of national security is not reorganization—it is getting our best people into key foreign policy and defense posts."

The clear assumption is that our best people are not in the government. If this is so, how are we to go about getting them into it? We do not believe in nor are we presently equipped to select youths, preferably superior ones, on a national basis for rigorous, prolonged training designed to prepare them for service as a governing elite.

Through our armed-service academies and war colleges, we do this for our military leadership. We accept and are rightly proud of the Marine Corps as an elite group. We accept and encourage the recognition of excellence and special status in the professions. But in the vital realm of civil administration we are ruggedly egalitarian. An attempt to create anything resembling the establishment would not only fail to get started but would be a national scandal.

It is not surprising that this is so. We have a long and assiduously cultivated tradition of disrespect for officialdom. We are suspicious of government. We feel that the country is great through the efforts of private citizens, in spite of the shenanigans of politicians and bureaucrats.

Because legislators are on the direct receiving end of public suspicion, their tendency is to kick the civil servant around at the end of a line of abuse. The politicians happily pander to the public conviction that government employees are wallowing in the public trough—in the case of the Foreign Service, up to their ears in whisky mash—and that few of them are capable of earning an honest day's living.

In this situation the public gets pretty much what it invites: a bulk of depressing mediocrity. To get a large body of talent, you have to pay for it in cash, prestige, and tenure.

By some strange quirk of human nature, the citizenry receives in some individual cases much better value than it invites, for there are in the mass of civil servants many of superior attainment and some who are absolutely first class. But there are not enough of them in the critical areas of government.

Without assurances of a fully rewarding career, we have failed to attract sufficient of the best talent when it is young. Consequently, we have tried to catch our best people when they are older, after they have sought and secured status in private endeavor. The assumption is that if a man has made his mark handling legal problems for large corporations or through manufacturing soap or by lecturing to postgraduates on political economy, he is by these credentials qualified to step into the management of the nation's affairs.

This legend derives from the implausible but nonetheless tenaciously held belief that administration of government is little different from and in any event not as exacting as moneymaking or pedagogy, and that it requires no apprenticeship or gradually acquired expertise as is the case in other careers.

Elihu Root, Henry Stimson, James Forrestal, and Robert Lovett are wistfully mentioned as models of what is sought in the citizen serving his country. They are what we need more of, it is said. Indeed, that is the case. But these are rare men, four over the span of as many decades. To be sure, there were and there are others from private life who served and now serve with wisdom and skill. They are, unhappily, the exceptional ones.

Mr. Lovett, former Under Secretary of State and later Secretary of Defense, told the Jackson subcommittee: "It takes a long time for an able man, without previous military service of some importance and experience in government, to catch up with his job in this increasingly complex Department [Defense]. At a guess, I would say he could pay good dividends to the Government in about two years."

Mr. Lovett is not recorded as having ventured an estimate of learning time for an able man in a top job in the Department of State dealing with foreign affairs, now so intricate as to require something close to extrasensory perception to comprehend any large part of it.

Stating the requirements in other terms, President Eisenhower in June, 1960, placed a four-year minimum for usefulness in "policy posts." Less than that would be "so brief as to minimize the value of the contribution and diminish the quality of public service."

It should not be assumed that all who volunteer or are drafted from private life for duties in the national interest forsake their accustomed occupations and stay on long enough to carry their own weight in positions of public trust. Some do. But for many, it is a transitory stint of public service.

How migratory our best people are in government is suggested by a 1958 survey made by the Harvard Business School Club of Washington which queried 456 businessmen who had between 1940 and 1956 joined the government and left it. Of this number, 48 per cent stayed one year or less. The average for all was one and one-quarter years.

Senator Jackson's subcommittee in 1960 found that seven different men had served as Secretary of Defense since the establishment of the post in 1947. Their average time on the job was less than two years. By 1964, Mr. McNamara raised the average to barely over the two years' minimum for learning.

Since the creation of the office of Deputy Secretary of Defense in 1949, nine men had occupied this position, averaging less than a year and a half. Here Mr. Gilpatric helped out slightly by enduring nearly three years. From 1949 to 1964, there were eight different Under Secretaries of State, averaging less than two years. The British opposite number, incidentally, is called the Permanent Under Secretary and is invariably from the career service on the humdrum theory that experience and know-how might be helpful.

The subcommittee also noted that a series of directors of the budget and chiefs of foreign aid had averaged less than two years each. When these escapees from Washington occur in close succession, the effect is rather impressive: the Department of Defense was abandoned in one six-month period by its Deputy Secretary, three Assistant Secretaries, and the General Counsel.

The restless passage of our best people through government recalls Mr. Lovett's estimate of two years of learning the job, assuming that the man is able. Dr. Herbert F. York, former director of defense research and engineering, testifying before the subcommittee, summed up the situation thus: "The average length of time a person holds his job, and this is not a new problem, is not really long enough to develop expertise at doing what needs to be done."

How do the affairs of state proceed in this parade of recurring amateurism? Assume an assistant secretary beginning his contribution to the commonweal, on leave from a real-estate operation in the sunland of the Southwest, meeting on an urgent problem with a special assistant, about to return to his academic chair at the end of two years of dedication to national security. The issue is urgent because officials of this stature do not have time to treat with nonurgent matters.

The Assistant Secretary is a man of action accustomed to making rapid-fire decisions on the basis of long-familiar business facts. He is not much given to reflection or to weighing abstractions. The Special Assistant is reflective and adept at abstractions, and during his months in government he has discovered that an appraisal followed by a conclusion, which sufficed in a seminar, must in the bureaucracy be confirmed by a decision to act, which must then be cleared with variable numbers of other officials and finally followed up by an "action-forcing process" to be sure that the action, with which he had had slight prior acquaintance, is taken.

This meeting represents the much-lauded cross-fertilization of ideas, bringing different points of view to bear on a single problem. It is popularly regarded as an absolute good, notwithstanding evidence from lower in the animal kingdom that only between a horse and an ass does cross-fertilization produce anything useful. As between our Assistant Secretary and our Special Assistant, disparate background, education, adult experience, vocabulary, and outlook assure a fairly nonproductive initial exchange.

Approaching the problem from different points of the compass, the conferees do not really join on the issue. If they are logical and patient and there is time for the exercise, there ensues a groping backward, step by step, in search of common basic assumptions. If those are found and identified, they can begin to build a structure of agreed-upon, relevant premises on which to judge the issue before them and decide on what to do.

But of course there is rarely time to bring order out of disorder. So the dialogue is resolved in a squidgy compromise or in a firm decision on infirm irrelevancies.

Our Assistant Secretary and our Special Assistant represent the simplest form of conference confusion. A committee or task force enriches the variety: a time-motion engineer from Detroit, temporarily with the Defense Department; a city hall reporter from the Northwest trying out Federal employment in the Voice of America; a Wall Street lawyer on leave to the Treasury and worrying about conflicts of interest; a union organizer on training tour in the Department of Labor; a 4H graduate from the Peace Corps; a politician unable to contain the fact that he is from the White House; and two middle-aged, inarticulate career officials, one a little chief from the Pentagon, the other an uprooted ambassador versed in Arabic affairs whose job had been given by the articulate politician from the White House to someone close to someone in the White House.

In this process of decision making, there is a central theme, as in a Pentecostal revival meeting. There is likewise the problem of intelligible communication, as when speaking with the gift of tongues.

It is in the efficiency of communication that an indoctrinated organization like the establishment does rather better. There is less of the blind men describing the elephant. The elephant has long since been categorized, perhaps even erroneously. Nevertheless, there is general agreement on the basic assumptions. So the conference point of departure is an estimate of the elephant's present disposition. Then, shall we prod the beast or should we feed him surplus peanuts? And if the decision is to prod, everyone concerned, already educated on the subject, knows pretty well, without a wealth of agonizing details laid out in a position paper, how, when, and where to prod. So, prodded the elephant is, and let the peanut surplus remain stored to the continuing benefit of the enterprising and the well connected.

Our tradition of turnover in government, which so troubled the Jackson subcommittee and others who have tangled with the problem, is of long standing. It goes back to the ceremony of throwing out the rascals with every change of political administration. This is based on the belief that while men may possibly grow in wisdom in office, it is sure that they grow in sloth and corruption. It is also based on greediness for spoils and payment for personal loyalty.

But the tradition of turnover goes even deeper. It goes to what Hamilton warned against. And here we have the full passage of what Hamilton wrote.

> To reverse and undo what has been done by a predecessor is very often considered by a successor as the best proof he can give of his own capacity and desert; and in addition to this propensity, where the alteration has been the result of public choice, the person substituted is warranted in supposing that the dismission of his predecessor has proceeded from a dislike to his measures; and that the less he resembles him, the more he will recommend himself to the favor of his constituents. These considerations, and the influence of personal confidences and attachments, would be likely to induce every new President to promote a change of men to fill the subordinate stations; and these causes together could not fail to occasion a disgraceful and ruinous mutability in the administration of the government.

Hamilton's forebodings have been fulfilled. The opportunity is irresistible. When the outs come in, there is a rite of spring, ousting the ins, disrupting the civil servants, and initiating the outs.

Such are the times of big turnover and maximum turmoil.

The career civil service tries, under the suspicious eyes of the newcomers with a mission, to keep the government running while the political appointees gradually become acquainted with one another, their jobs, and how to get things done in a bureaucracy.

The New York Times reported on April 16, 1962, that the government had drawn up an overall strategic plan and that "completion of the master plan was deferred until the second year of the Kennedy Administration to give various agencies and officials time to learn their function and to test their policy ideas." Meanwhile events in the rest of the world had not been marking time waiting for us to compose ourselves.

The gypsy-encampment atmosphere along the banks of the Potomac usually settles somewhat in the second year of a new administration, but by then there has begun the turnover among the newcomers.

The Democratic dispensation in 1961 was no exception. Before three years had passed, it had its third Secretary of the Navy. The first was lured by Texas politics; the second left amidst a typical Washington flurry involving a code of ethics for high officials, a scandal over aircraft procurement, the use of Navy stationery, and Texans invited to cruise on a yacht.

Less baffling were square-peg to squarish-hole shifts by the Under Secretary of State and the Counselor of said department. But neither quite fitted in the new slots, so by 1963 both had been moved to other openings.

The Secretary of the Army found that he preferred the University of Indiana and left before a year and a half had passed. And in a rather novel transaction, some two hundred senior Foreign Service officers were brought into premature retirement in mid-1962, while there continued the politicization of the Department of State with pedagogues and politicians.

The directors of the Bureau of the Budget and of the foreign-aid program maintained the past average of time on the job by moving out of their offices in less than two years. By the third year of the Kennedy administration the President had lost three of his Cabinet, Ribicoff, Goldberg, and Day, to the Senate, the Supreme Court, and the practice of law.

Sometimes the moves in government are in the back-and-forth manner of a shuttle weaving from a tangled skein. Take the case of William H. Orrick, Jr., a graduate of Yale and a socially prominent San Francisco lawyer. He helped to elect John F. Kennedy to the presidency and, in the process, so impressed Robert F. Kennedy with his vigor that in 1961 he was drawn to Washington as Assistant Attorney General in charge of the civil division of the Justice Department. Unafflicted by cultural shock, he adapted to walking three miles to office, scorning elevators to bound up stairways and working for photographers in his galluses, sleeves rolled to biceps, collar unbuttoned, tie knotted at collarbone, and fist full of papers.

But alas, poor Orrick. Justice knew him not well. And vice versa. For there was not time to become more than barely acquainted before he was shifted. His boss, whose concerns transcended Justice, relinquished his Civil assistant in 1962 to get State moving. Orrick was put in charge of administration, personnel, finances, and establishments, the physical operations of the largest foreign-affairs enterprise in the world—the catacombs at Foggy Bottom, plus more than 100 embassies, legations, and special missions and over 180 consular offices.

Nor did this last long. Before mid-1963, having failed to bust State, he was back at Justice as chief trustbuster, not in the job about which he had begun to learn something two years before. He was quoted as saying that he was glad to be "back in the family."

The customary derangement of the executive is aggravated when the Congress interests itself in executive matters. Much of this intervention is legitimate and ultimately constructive. Particularly useful is the budget process and what Mr. Lovett called the legislature's "performance audit" of the administration. But this is only so when the congressional intervention is within proper bounds. When it is excessive, the effect is not only disruptive and wasteful; it can be demoralizing.

Such abuse was foreseen by Hamilton in 1778. He remarked on

> the tendency of the legislative authority to absorb every other. . . . The representatives of the people, in a popular assembly, seem sometimes to fancy that they are the people themselves, and betray strong symptoms of impatience and disgust at the least sign of opposition from any other quarter; as if the exercise of its rights, by either the executive or judiciary, were a breach of their privilege and an outrage to their dignity. They often appear disposed to exert an imperious control over the other departments.

Often it is our best people and the miserable bureaucrats who are caught in the middle when there is a violation of the separation of powers. Walter Lippmann described what happens when a particularly aggressive attempt is made by a member or committee of the Congress to "invade and usurp" the executive:

> It destroys the spirit and morale and efficiency of civil servants. When this condition prevails, men work with one eye on their official boss and the other eye on the inquisitors from Congress. Temptation is great to feed out information, rumors and innuendo behind the official boss's back, either to curry the favor of the inquisitor or to placate his wrath. Subordinates cannot count on being protected against public degradation and the boss cannot count on his staff to serve him loyally.

It is not a lemming instinct that draws outsiders into the government. It is usually something quite mixed. Part of it, and in many cases the dominant motivation, is a genuine desire to serve the country. There is also the wish to improve one's chances for a still better status in private life, using the government as a steppingstone thereto.

For the older man who has enjoyed success in his business or profession, government may be a new field to conquer, a laurel wreath of crowning adventure and honor. And of course there is always the mama for whom government is glamorous, especially if papa can afford a Georgetown garden with boxwood hedges or a swank ambassadorship.

Why do these people leave the government? Most of them regard their stay in executive office as temporary, if for no other reason than that they are politically appointed and subject to the cyclical changes of politics. Some, however, submerge themselves in the civil service, take on nonpartisan coloration, develop a valuable expertise, and survive changes of administration.

The exodus of many, as has been noted, is accelerated so that the tenure of office is considerably less than the minimum of four years for usefulness recommended by President Eisenhower. The causes of this differ. In some cases the chance for self-improvement back in the private sector or in politics comes early and is grasped without delay. In other instances there quickly develop policy differences, incompatibilities, or frustrations with a baffling bureaucracy. And then there are those who, feeling that the gaff that must be withstood and the guff that must be taken are rather beyond the call of civic duty, quietly fold their tents and return to decent, self-respecting privacy.

We would not entrust any segment of our personal affairs to an institution, whether bank, hospital, or school, managed in the manner that our collective security and wellbeing are administered. We have gotten away with governmental disarray because the private sector of our American society is enormously rich and productive and has thus far been able to support this extravagance. We have made do through sheer economic and military muscle, not through skill and efficient management of our affairs.

The public indulgence of government by recurring waves of diminishing ignorance may have been acceptable when we dwelt in relative isolation. It is now a perilously sloppy procedure. Irrespective of the Soviet challenge, we owe it to ourselves in self-respect and in the knowledge of our ever-expanding responsibilities in foreign and domestic matters to put the management of our affairs in better order.

This does not mean, of course, that we should throw overboard our political mores and try to adopt a rigid system like the mandarinate or least of all the apparatus. Such an attempt would be out of character, undesirable, and impossible.

It does mean that we should adopt a less flighty approach to government. What is needed is continuity and a high level of professional competence.

The Cabinet and heads of most agencies should, quite evidently, be political appointees, sensitive from the outset to the President's thinking and wishes. A few politically chosen lieutenants might be introduced into each department. But there should not be, at least in the key departments and agencies, a constant coming and going of crusading amateurs. This will be hard on new presidents and on the national committees, who invariably contract more political debts than they can discharge. But on the theory that the country is more important than the party, this should be done.

Knowing what should be done and doing it are two different things. Whether we can develop efficient management of the nation's affairs depends on the public—whether it is disposed to demand that the politicians in the executive and the politicians in the legislature create the conditions that will permit efficiency. The bureaucracy itself is not the major problem. It can be improved in quality, as it needs to be, if the preconditions are there; otherwise not.

Disgraceful and Ruinous Mutability?

If the public comes to believe that its welfare and security require excellence and continuity in the administration of public affairs under the direction of an elected chief executive, the next question is whether it will pay the cost of excellence, whether it will grant the intangible reward of prestige and the tangible one of salaries comparable to those in the privileged professions.

Beyond this, it must be asked whether the public will accept that, in return for nonpartisanship by the bureaucracy, the civil servant should not be involved in what Mr. Lippmann referred to as "a recurrent phenomenon in our political history"—the attempts by the Congress to "invade and usurp" the executive.

Do the people and its legislators accept this judgment? And will they pay the cost of excellence in the civil service?

The answer is—not now.

The public, with its ingrained suspicion of bureaucrats, will not be willing to pay for excellence in the management of its collective affairs in the present atmosphere. As for the politicians, they have so deep a vested interest in perpetuating political favors and spoils and so strong a tradition of open-season hunting of the bureaucrat that they will be loath to deny themselves these perquisites of elected office. Finally, the inclination is not to make any extensive change of this character until jarred into doing so by disaster.

The habitual dissipation in the operation of the Federal Government will, therefore, continue. Meanwhile the vitality and strength of the private sector will still support and overshadow the malfunctioning of public administration.

In our rapidly changing society and world, however, with increasing power gravitating to government, we cannot be sure that the present balance will last indefinitely.

So the "mutability in the administration of government" is disgraceful, yes. But ruinous, not yet.

Above All Zeal

*I*t was possible as
late as 1936 to encompass all the Washington personnel of
the Department of State in one photograph.

In those days, when there were about three score independent countries in the world, the conduct of our foreign
relations was a good deal quieter. Those were the interwar
years when we tended to stay out of other people's affairs.
When we did intervene as a government, and that was rarely,
it was usually on behalf of American business interests.

We were aware of injustice, misery, and aggression
abroad, but with the exception of Japan's invasion of Manchuria, we did not feel called upon to act (and then ineffec-
tually) in resistance to aggression. Nor did we feel that it
was incumbent upon our government to improve the lot of
alien peoples.

Relations with other nations were conducted principally
through conventional diplomatic channels. Diplomacy, the
management of international relations by negotiation, was
limited in scope to the traditional concerns of commerce,
navigation, finance, the protection of American nationals,
treaty observance, and chasing narcotics smugglers. The

staffs of the Department of State and of embassies, legations, and consulates abroad were mostly professional in character and modest in size.

Charles Evans Hughes and Henry L. Stimson were left to direct American foreign affairs without volunteer assists from officials whose primary responsibilities lay elsewhere. Even generals and admirals hesitated to issue pronouncements on explosive political issues.

It was under the administration of Franklin D. Roosevelt and in response to the demands of global war that proliferated diplomacy came into flower. It began with the President preferring to undercut rather than replace Cordell Hull, and with the creation of new functions having to do with our foreign relations: lend-lease, economic warfare, propaganda, secret operations, relief and rehabilitation. Large bureaucracies were assembled to administer these activities, more or less (usually less) under the coordination of the Secretary of State. Semisecretaries of State sprang up in the White House and in the new agencies: Harry Hopkins, Lauchlin Currie, Wild Bill Donovan, Donald Nelson, Robert Sherwood. The Vice President, Henry Wallace establishing a precedent that has been upheld by some of his successors, goodwilled in South America and troubleshot in Asia. Except for two trips overseas, Mr. Hull stayed in Washington trying to keep track of what his competitors were up to.

With peace, there began a demobilization of this colorful equipage. But then we came to see that our ally, the Soviet Union, was really our mortal enemy. And later we concluded that our former enemies had become essential allies.

So cold war soon replaced hot war. Foreign-aid programs lent, leased, relieved, rehabilitated, and granted; USIA spoke where OWI had been heard; CIA improved on the lessons of OSS; and military advisory groups appeared where once there had been expeditionary forces. The freewheeling bureaucracies reappeared and flourished.

By now the conduct of foreign relations is well established as everyone's business. With the Peace Corps in the act, butchers, bakers, and candlestick makers are eligible. There has never been such wide mobilization of if not talent at least bodies to deal with what has hitherto been regarded as a delicate and specialized undertaking—managing our relations with other countries.

The range of our recent official effort is arresting. A random sampling of only our itinerant representation reveals: the vice-presidents of the United States (Nixon and Johnson), the Holiday on Ice troupe, Joey Adams, the Attorney General, Louis "Satchmo" Armstrong, Mr. Justice Douglas, the Secretary of Labor, the AAU Weight Lifting Team, James Hagerty and Pierre Salinger of the White House, and the Harlem Globetrotters and the congressional globetrotters. It is not for want of contacts that foreigners perversely continue to perplex and provoke us.

Diplomacy is now not only everybody's business; it is also big business, very big business. It is big money, big programs, big operations, big staffs. Its spirit was voiced by Fowler Hamilton who, after being sworn in as foreign-aid administrator in 1961, was reported to have announced with the expansiveness of a public figure rather than with the precision of a lawyer that he proposed to run the foreign-aid program like "the $4,000,000,000 enterprise it is."

What we are engaged in is intervention. It is the new intervention, a new dollar diplomacy where the dollar is given, rather than taken, where we press our surplus grain and our short-supply gold on the recipients for their obvious gain and our putative benefit.

The new intervention attempts also to be opinion-forming abroad. Reacting to the worldwide ideological offensive of the Communists, we have joined battle for men's minds in alien lands. Thus government has embarked upon proselytization of foreigners, which had hitherto been viewed as a fit and proper activity for private citizens and organizations but inappropriate for the government.

What we seek to buy and propagandize with the new intervention is a national state of mind in the "target" countries. Of course countries have been bought before. They have been bought through bribing the king, the chief minister, the junta, or those who manipulated the votes. But we are attempting to buy and persuade into being economic, political, and social conditions in foreign states, conditions that will at least permit, or better spontaneously create, a mass mentality resistant to Soviet blandishment, menace, and trickery.

Social engineering of this breadth and depth would be an ambitious undertaking in our own society and would arouse widespread opposition. Directed at peoples differing from us in varying measures, and from one another, the new intervention is a less than modest proposition. Especially is this so when so many of those planning and implementing the programs are only superficially acquainted with formative forces in the "target" countries.

What is lacking in perception is more than made up in activity. Characteristic of the new intervention is a philosophy of activism, a belief in the efficacy of works. Since the results sought are amorphous, an indiscriminate range of activities can be and is represented as contributing to the desired ends. Uninhibited by deep understanding of the peoples affected, everything from dams and bazookas to home economics and Bach is held forth as efficacious against communism and so as contributive to the security of the United States.

An effort of this diffuse magnitude naturally produces bureaucratic gargantuanism, for inconsequentialities, too, require their staffs in Washington and abroad. It may be that bigness is neutral, neither good nor bad. It is certain that organizational turgidity in the conduct of our foreign relations is a cause of inefficiency and prodigality.

The sheer volume of the activity is such that it is bound to be cargoed with trivia. Considering the Department of State and not the agencies also involved in foreign affairs, it alone, according to the Secretary, received and sent in 1961 some two thousand telegrams a day. Does the traffic in matters instantaneously or even ultimately significant to American national interest equal the telegraphic traffic? One would suspect not.

Carlton Savage of the Department's Policy Planning Council pled in October, 1961, for a condensation of the cable dialogue of the new diplomacy so that the President and the Secretary might have more time for other activities. The exchange between Washington and the field, he pointed out, totaled fifty million words a year. The daily average of this is equivalent in bulk, if not sense and style, to the books of Genesis, Exodus, Numbers, Job, Song of Solomon, and Lamentations.

In 1963, a Senate committee revealed that the daily average of this headlong traffic was three hundred thousand words. This was double the volume that had so dismayed Mr. Savage two years before.

In addition to the electrified discourse, there is the plodding output and intake of mail communications, memorandums, and research studies by the Department of State, the agencies (including the copious Central Intelligence Agency), and the private research corporations. State Department couriers moving this precious cargo to and from posts abroad log nine million miles a year, equivalent to eight round trips to the moon. There is an indigestible abundance of raw material on which to base decisions—the Bay of Pigs venture alone suggests that not all the information that we gather at considerable expense is dependable.

An attempt is being made to process the welter of "facts" on foreign affairs by computers so as to ease decision making. We should wish well to this try at automated diplomacy. If, unhappily, it should fail, the government will be forced to depend upon human discrimination, a capacity to tell the significant from the trivial or false.

Characteristic of the new diplomacy is a preoccupation on the part of many of its practitioners with the personal image. Imagery, however, is not new to diplomacy. Benjamin Franklin made his ploy about clothing at the French court, ever since a favorite gambit. And Charles Gates

Dawes refused to wear knee breeches at the Court of St. James's.

Imagery is now institutionalized, with staffs dedicated to and having a vested interest in cosmeticizing public personalities, political, military, and diplomatic. When the statesman himself is gifted in this respect, the production is a work of art.

So it should cause no surprise, while in search of information from the printed page, to find oneself face to open face with an Assistant Secretary of State shaking hands with an African digging in a ditch somewhere on the Dark Continent. What is the message of such a tableau? The Assistant Secretary is democratic, he is a bearcat on the job, and he goes after the facts at the source. What is its significance in the conduct of foreign relations? Precious little, for the recipient of this high-level diplomatic attention and his like is politically nearly meaningless.

One of the most creative practitioners of imagery was the eminent scholar-ambassador to India who had himself photographed in 1961 with his prop—an Indian peasant woman in a paddy field. The professor-diplomat was, of course, shaking hands with the startled female ryot, indicating in the routine manner a friendly, straightforward personality. But better than having his sleeves rolled up (the conventional symbol for devotion to duty), his pants were rolled up and he was barefoot, ankle-deep in the hookworm culture of the paddy field. This was inspired imagery, an unforgettable revelation of diplomacy hard at it at the rice-roots level. Not revealed in the photograph was His Excellency's tongue, deftly concealed in his cheek.

Foreign and Other Affairs

A more exuberant exhibition for the lenses was the do-all-for-Udall school. This is the public show of sheer physical prowess and endurance: climbing Fujiyama and Kilimanjaro and other romantic foreign mountains. It is unlikely proof that a man is a statesman, else we should have a Cabinet of Sherpas. But it does rate full-page spreads in *Life* and wows the electorate.

In addition to the conventional symbols of handshakes and rolled-up sleeves, there are animals. Theodore Roosevelt favored dead ones, freshly shot on safari. The other Roosevelt used them alive, in the case of Falla to striking political effect. The Nixon cocker, Checkers, was a moving symbol of domestic felicity, although not mobilized in Richard Nixon's foreign campaigns.

Foreign crowds were Mr. Nixon's real meat, whether as Vice President or privately keeping in the public eye. He mingled his way across Asia mystifying the Mystic East with oratory in a tongue unknown to the multitudes. His successor, Lyndon Johnson, as Vice President, later went over the same circuit with a folksier performance. In South Vietnam, he reportedly likened President Ngo Dinh Diem to Lincoln and in Karachi managed to convey to a bewildered camel driver an invitation to visit the LBJ ranch in Texas.

Bashir Ahmed took the invitation seriously and after thinking it over for some days accepted, to the then Vice President's initial discomfort but subsequent gratification— the camel driver became an instantaneous celebrity, causing the LBJ image to glow with a benign reflected light. Notwithstanding the incandescent goodwill generated by this fraternization, relations between the United States and Pakistan later went into a decline.

President Kennedy's triumphal tours abroad were favored by no better ultimate results. During his first year in office, he visited de Gaulle and Khrushchev, following which their policies toward the United States hardened. He went to Ottawa. Anti-Americanism subsequently grew in Canada. He went in 1963 to Central America and shortly thereafter came the first of a series of military coups in Latin America. He went to Western Europe to revitalize the grand design only to come back to the drawing boards at 1600 Pennsylvania Avenue.

It is not that there is a cause and effect relationship between these occurrences. It is only that elaborate exposure of our public personages does not really alter very much the course of events.

Most American political figures, when they see a crowd, even though a collection of alien faces, revert to type. They are swept by an uncontrollable desire to electioneer, like Kennedy's *"Ich bin ein Berliner."* The wildly cheering multitude, however, was made up not of his constituents but of Willy Brandt's. Compulsive international barnstorming, in sum, keeps the vision of statesmanship luminous at home but is usually of ephemeral benefit to American national interest. This is so whether the crowds are friendly, indifferent, or diverted.

When the reception is hostile, some seek to rise above the discord, as James Hagerty did in Tokyo, with a leg-up from a helicopter. Others choose to go in search of a mob, as Mr. Nixon did in his Lima crisis, and debate with it via the detours of an interpreter, and so thrust the goodwill mission upon a fanatical fringe determined to reject it and capitalize on that rejection.

This may be a role for a religious or a political zealot welcoming martyrdom; it is hardly one for a high official of the United States. The personal crisis in Lima did not set back Communism in Peru, which has since increased in strength. It did, however, add a silver lining of heroism to the personal image back home.

Less splashy but also image making in a way were Robert F. Kennedy's café seminars in Japan and debates in Indonesia with intellectually curious students. In the latter the Attorney General was reported to have confessed that perhaps we had erred in taking Texas from Mexico. He denied that he had done any such thing, claiming that he spoke not of the War of Texan Independence but of that of 1846–48. So presumably no offer was made to give the Lone Star State back to the Mexicans, a prospect which could have been no less appalling to the supposed beneficiaries than to those who would be retroceded. In any event this skirmish in the battle for men's minds, whatever effect it may have had on dialectically inclined Indonesians, did produce a definite image of the Attorney General back in Texas.

These particular excursions of the Attorney General into Mr. Rusk's and Mr. Murrow's troubled domains appear to have been prompted by the discovery of a long-standing, widespread phenomenon: procommunism and anti-Americanism among many voluble students abroad. Mr. Kennedy undertook personally to assure young Asians that the United States was still vital and on the move, while the Marxist system was experiencing serious failures. In Djakarta, as later in the Hague, he also made a stab at mediating on New Guinea. And in Germany, in company with his brother Edward (then qualifying for high office in the United States by hobnobbing with foreigners), he met with Dr. Adenauer. The Attorney General also broadcast to the East Germans a message of contingent hope for a possible liberalization of their yoke.

The total image from these activities in early 1962 was confused because of its very diffusion, especially when compounded with his other excursions overseas. It lacked the in-focus clarity of Henry Wallace's highly personalized throwing of the boomerang, cross-country hikes, and ball tossing. The results of the Attorney General's straying into foreign affairs appear to have been even slighter than Mr. Wallace's vaults into diplomacy.

What can be said is that, in finding out how critical foreigners were of the treatment of Negroes in the United States, the Attorney General's attention was drawn back to his proper sphere of duties, thus preparing him a little for the shock of later discovering the enormous dilemma of racialism lying in wait for him at home.

But one must draw the veil somewhere, and in so doing it is perhaps permissible to state that all the export imagery finds a fertile environment in the new diplomacy. It flourishes in the big-business, big-operations, big-staffs soil. It is fertilized by all-purpose, homogenized intervention in other people's affairs. And it blooms in the tropical atmosphere of activism and opinion-forming among strangers.

Notwithstanding its drawbacks, the new diplomacy is

here to stay. It will, one must believe, mature. But the conduct of our foreign relations can no more revert to the substance and style of Elihu Root and Charles Evans Hughes than could that of the mid-war years to the diplomacy as administered by John Quincy Adams on behalf of James Monroe. With a discriminating economy of effort, this representative of the early American elite managed our foreign affairs in a time of turmoil and revolution with one chief clerk, nine clerks, and two messengers—thirteen slots in all.

While the new diplomacy is by way of becoming a permanent mode, it need not be so inept, extravagant, and overblown. Fortunately there has been recognition of this, at least by the Senate's subcommittee on national policy machinery. Senator Jackson, chairman of that body, concluded in November, 1961, that "no task is more urgent than improving the effectiveness of the Department of State."

He also pointed out that we needed a clearer understanding of where our vital national interests lay, that there was serious overstaffing in the national security departments and agencies, and that the heart problem lay in the quality of the men doing the job. "Poor decisions," the Senator observed, "are traceable not to machinery but to people—to their inexperience, their failure to comprehend the full significance of information crossing their desks, to their indecisiveness or lack of wisdom."

What the Senator seemed to be looking for was the quality of discrimination, for with it, a clearer understanding of where our vital national interests lie should be less difficult to come by.

But the senatorial quest was apparently to little avail. A philosophy of bronco-busting activism continued to dominate the new diplomacy. In 1963, two years after the Jackson evaluation, the then Under Secretary for Political Affairs, George McGhee, in portraying the ideal, the gung-ho ambassador, exclaimed: "He must be a man who can get the job done—a man with a sense of urgency, a man whom nothing defeats, a man who 'can do' in the best and most traditionally American sense of that phrase."

As for the overstaffing that concerned the Senator, deficiency of discrimination produces gargantuanism in our government in two respects. It tolerates and even creates undertakings not really advancing the vital national interests. The executive types currently in favor, conditioned to operational criteria rather than substantive evaluation, are not the answer to these extravagances. It also means too many men on the job, for one man with the capacity to discriminate is worth many without it, assuming that those without are benign factors and not contraproductive. Rounding out the vicious circle, bureaucratic bloat encourages lack of discrimination.

Were this quality of selective perception applied, the staffs dealing with foreign affairs would be cut to a fraction of their present girth. Similarly, many activities and expenditures in the conduct of our foreign relations would be reduced or eliminated.

But discrimination is not a natural talent generously bestowed. And its development through rigorous training and experience is attained in diplomacy over a span of years.

Discrimination in the conduct of foreign relations starts with a native perceptiveness and sensitivity. If these inborn qualities are absent, no amount of training or experience will compensate. As a subsequently developed faculty, it embraces a knowledge and sense of history; an insight into diverse foreign psychologies gained through experience; a developing sense of proportion, and thereby a sense of humor about relations among peoples and governments; and from these, some understanding of the limits of power, the fallibility of one's own judgments, the stubbornness of traditional ways and beliefs, the greater persuasiveness of example over words, the uses of implicit rather than explicit force, the value of frequent silence, the worth of occasional inaction, and the need for constant patience.

In its most highly developed form, discrimination is also intuitive. We understand this in domestic politics. Because international affairs are at once more intricate and diffuse, intuition is an even more valuable attribute in diplomacy—when it is educated and not merely inspired.

It is too much to expect that the lawyers, politicians, bankers, newsmen, generals, professors, and others who lend their services temporarily to the needs of American diplomacy should all have a background and flair for the conduct of foreign relations. A few do and, after a year or two of learning, make a useful and occasionally brilliant contribution, following which they withdraw.

So this group is not the answer to Senator Jackson's plea for "improving the effectiveness of the Department of State." This is so if for no other reason than that the practitioners of *diplomatus interruptus* are, generally speaking, creative only accidentally.

Nor has the career Foreign Service been what the Senator called for. It has been fashionable to say that the Foreign Service suffered from stagnation. It is more accurate to say that it suffered from shock.

Consider the case history. Because it deals with suspect matters like foreigners, strange languages, and diplomacy, the Foreign Service is, to an accentuated degree, subjected to the popular distrust of and distaste for bureaucrats.

The Foreign Service has sometimes been likened to an elite group. This has never been anything but a crassly superficial appraisal, confusing the tedium of social functions with privilege, official title with authority, and, silliest of all, the lubricating civilities of protocol with activities subversive to the self-respect of red-blooded citizens—like eating snails.

The fact of the matter is that since the end of the 1920s the Foreign Service has been increasingly egalitarian. Then in the late forties and early fifties it was tinkered with and overhauled by a succession of commissions and administrative manipulators determined to make it over into the closest mathematical equivalent of the average middle-class citizenry. The theory was that the Foreign Service officer should be representative. In practice it meant pressure toward mediocrity rather than toward being representative of the higher accomplishments of our civilization.

Such were the efforts to make a group of for the most part already rather unremarkable talent and ability even more ordinary. Notwithstanding these leveling endeavors, the beginnings of self-imposed standards of intellectual excellence and indications of élan were discernible in the Foreign Service. They were almost underground, but they existed.

The attacks from the radical right, culminating in the

early fifties, destroyed this striving toward distinction and a personality in the Foreign Service. The violence and subtlety of the purge and intimidation left the Foreign Service demoralized and intellectually cowed. With some doughty exceptions, it became a body of conformists. The timidity influenced promotions, and many cautious mediocrities rose to the top of the Service.

Then came the New Frontiersmen. Bold new ideas and quick decisions were asked of men who had learned from long, disillusioning experience that there were few or no new ideas, bold or otherwise, that would solidly produce the dramatic changes then sought, and whose experience for a decade had been that bold ideas and actions were personally dangerous and could lead to congressional investigations and public disgrace. The Foreign Service was also told to get out and get to know the opposition in foreign countries, when experience or example had taught that acquaintance with oppositionists at any time, even twenty years earlier, had been the cause for "loyalty hearings."

The New Frontiersmen were disappointed with the response of the Foreign Service to the clarion call to action. So there took place another, but genteel, purge, this time from the liberal center.

That the Foreign Service did not win the confidence of the New Frontiersmen is not surprising. Crusading activism touched with naïveté seldom welcomes warnings of pitfalls and entanglements. What is a pity is that the Foreign Service did not win their respect.

As a professional corps created to do the job, it had education and experience, but, with a few outstanding exceptions, it lacked stature. It lacked stature because the nascent demand for excellence and the flair and the élan of the late 1940s had been gutted. That is where the Foreign Service failed, as it had itself been failed.

Time will give the new generation in the Foreign Service, less affected by the mid-century debacle, the opportunity to show whether it has learned discrimination and acquired a vigorous personality, able to ride out the inevitable next concentrated assault upon it, meanwhile making a creative and courageous contribution.

Much will depend upon the men at the top of the Service, whether they will be permitted to and if so whether they can and will teach, train, drill, exact from, and inspire their subordinates. The productive relationship in diplomatic training is still one of master and apprentice. Only thus will the Service come to excel and acquire a sustaining esprit de corps.

Time will also reveal changes abroad, beyond our control, which should in turn temper the new diplomacy. As Europe's individuality has emerged and asserted itself, avuncular expressions of policy by us toward the Western European countries have become patently ridiculous and our interventionist activities as unwarranted as they are unwelcome.

The underdeveloped countries will seek increasingly to manifest independence of us and of the Kremlin, even while continuing to be economically dependent upon playing us (and Europe) off one against the other. We will become more aware of the limitations of what we alone, or in partnership with Europe, can do in creating wealth and democracy where the preconditions do not exist. We will also come to recognize, if our society remains dynamic, the declining appeal of the Soviet Union (but not necessarily communist theory) to the underdeveloped countries. Consequently in these nations, too, events are likely to give reason for diminishing the new dollar diplomacy, social engineering, and proselytization in which we are now so anxiously engaged.

The Congress, in its role as auditor of foreign policy, will play a critical role in these readjustments. Fortunately, senators of the caliber of Fulbright, Mansfield, and Hickenlooper have long experience in monitoring international affairs. There are, of course, still those like the congressman on one of the immediate postwar junkets of Europe who had all of the glib answers on big international issues, hedged on what was happening in American national politics, and threw up his hands as too complicated to explain the situation in his congressional district.

Our hope must be that the Congress, too, will mature and, as Senator Jackson urged, put its own house in better order. If the legislators who during the past decade have been moving about the world quietly and seriously can make their wisdom felt among their colleagues less experienced in foreign affairs, the Congress may play a more constructive role than the executive in moderating the conduct of our foreign relations.

Moderation does not mean a futile effort to return to the old diplomacy which, too, had its serious faults. It means recognizing that in the conduct of our foreign relations we are grossly overextended physically, emotionally, and intellectually—and then acting upon the obvious conclusions to be drawn therefrom.

In Search
of Monsters

*F*rom Green-
land's icy mountains to India's coral strand, for a century
and a half, thousands of Americans have struggled to propa-
gate the faith and convert the heathen. It was, and still is, a
selfless, dedicated commitment to change the beliefs and lives
of other men.

This labor of persuasion was from the beginning regarded
as belonging within what is now fashionably called the private sector, for the American government had no role in the
proselytization of foreigners.

Only a generation ago, the general inclination was that,
as a nation, we should mind our own business. In the public
sector, the United States "has abstained from interference
in the concerns of others," said John Quincy Adams, "even
when the conflict has been for principles to which she clings,
as to the last vital drop that visits the heart."

Recognizing that this was a Fourth of July oration but
not taking it, in our manner, as mere bombast because of
that, we would do well by our sense of perspective to listen
to some of the other things Mr. Adams had to say.

Wherever the standard of freedom and independence has been and shall be unfurled, there will her heart, her benedictions, and her prayers be. But she goes not abroad in search of monsters to destroy. She is the well-wisher to the freedom and independence of all. She is the champion and vindicator only of her own. She will recommend the general cause by the countenance of her voice, and the benignant sympathy of her example. She well knows that by once enlisting under other banners than her own, were they even the banners of foreign independence, she would involve herself beyond the power of extrication, in all the wars of interest and intrigue, of individual avarice, envy and ambition, which assume the colors and usurp the standard of freedom. . . . She might become the dictatress of the world. She would be no longer the ruler of her own spirit.

Mr. Adams and some of the other gentlemen who got us going as a nation were shrewd judges of human nature, including our own. They were far too perceptive to become infatuated by the surface phenomena they saw abroad. And they modestly understood the limitations of what we could do beyond our own jurisdiction and the dangers of overreaching ourselves.

Another Bostonian, 141 years later, in his 1962 State of the Union Message, proclaimed: "People everywhere, in spite of occasional disappointments, look to us—not to our wealth or power, but to the splendor of our ideals. For our nation is commissioned by history to be either an observer of freedom's failure or the cause of its success."

History had here acquired alien godlike attributes. Proselytization had swelled from spiritual to secular concern, from private consecration to public function. The Federal

Government was ordained by history to busy itself with saving the political heathen in foreign lands, converting them by example and by good works from the sin of unrepresentative government.

We were told that foreigners looked to us for leadership. It was our mission to inspire people in distant lands with the revolutionary impact of American life, achievement, and dreams so that they would cherish freedom and embrace the idea of a world community of harmonious, independent states, as envisaged in the United Nations Charter.

This is a large and diffuse undertaking for a government. And proselytization by bureaucracy is new to us. The general proposition of trying to inspire foreigners with a revolutionary idea is, however, as old as the Christian missionary movement. Many of the government's opinion-forming techniques, which may seem to be innovations, are well established in the history of the church's activities in foreign fields. The experiences of the past in inspiration and persuasion illuminate the groping efforts of the present.

In the sixteenth century the first Jesuits arrived in China. They were tolerated and finally accepted by the suspicious, archaic court at Peking, more because of their representation of the life and achievements of the West than for their religion. Matteo Ricci, the leader of the group, was a scholar and by all accounts a man of exceptional stature. He and his successors tactfully avoided contesting Confucian rites for somewhat the same reasons that our policy now is to avoid condemning neutralism as immoral. Imputations of immorality usually leave the listener unmoved, unless to the disadvantage of the moralist.

Anticipating the activities of our cultural attachés and information officers, these Jesuits brought and later published books and expounded on Western accomplishments and dreams. Like our aid missions, they introduced Western scientific knowledge and techniques and told of Occidental methods of education. And in the manner of a Military Assistance Advisory Group, they taught the Chinese how to cast brass cannon.

For three and a half centuries Catholic and then Protestant missionaries in China propagated not only the Christian faith but also the Western point of view: individualism, human rights, and, from the nineteenth century onward, freedom. They also taught the Western way of doing things: the scientific method, mechanization, and technology.

Dwarfing our present worldwide governmental programs in effort, if not cash, expended, this private-sector proselytization had in China during the third decade of this century more than ten thousand American and European missionaries in person-to-person programs, over a hundred Christian colleges and universities, some seven hundred high schools, more than four thousand primary schools, and in excess of five hundred hospitals and clinics.

In mass media, the output was prodigious. Catholic production alone in secular matters included thirteen scientific periodicals and forty-nine dealing with social, cultural, and educational subjects. In addition to their own publications, the Protestants opened in 1936 a radio station.

Our student-exchange programs have their precedents in the thousands of Chinese students who for at least two generations went to the United States and Western Europe for higher education. Many of them became the leaders in the "modernization" of China.

All of this was done not without sacrifice. Most readily there comes to mind the 221 missionary men, women, and children slaughtered in the Boxer Rebellion. More recently, in the five years 1929–1934, bandits or Communists kidnapped or killed fifty-four missionaries.

What came of this prolonged outpouring of love, labor, and blood?

Less than 1 per cent of the population of China was converted to Christianity. China was but superficially modernized and was torn by dissension. The massive bulk of Chinese existed in a Malthusian cycle, illiterate, impoverished, and fatalistic.

Then came the culmination. Three hundred and fifty years of enlightenment from the West was extinguished by an ideological movement that had existed in China for less than thirty years. Communism then undertook the modernization of China by force.

But this is only part of the object lesson for us. There was also Japan. There the impact of the West had a revolutionary effect. Shortly after Commodore Perry "opened" Japan, the Japanese themselves began, in 1868, the Meiji Reformation. In a little more than thirty years, they had made themselves enough of a power to challenge the Russian Empire and then defeat it on land and sea.

In this underdeveloped country the example of Western life and achievements, the instruction of missionaries, and the education of young Japanese in the West created a revolution, as it had not in China. In one generation, Japan was well on the way to modernization and status as a world power.

The Japanese continued on this course, selecting from the West what they calculated would add to their power, commercially, industrially, politically, and militarily. That from the West for which they felt no need, they slighted or ignored. Less than half of 1 per cent of the Japanese adopted Christianity.

The culmination of Japan's eager acceptance of Western life and achievements was Pearl Harbor. After defeating the Japanese, we imposed on them, through military occupation and rule, democracy and a recognition of the values of freedom and of a world community of harmonious and independent states, as laid down in the UN Charter.

There should be some lessons for the present out of this past. One lesson is that opinion-forming will probably fail if what we have to say is not, in the mind of our audience, relevant to its own situation. That was one of the great problems with the Chinese. As Confucianists, the idea of salvation was implausible; as Buddhists, it seemed unnecessary. Individualism was meaningless, when not shameful, in a civilization rooted in the family system. Human rights and freedom had long ago been appropriately delineated by Confucius; any fault lay with the misdeeds of the magistrate, and it would be unseemly for a barbarian, however well-intentioned, to speak out boldly in such matters.

As for the mechanical contrivances of the West, entertaining, useful, and desirable—but how to create large mechanized enterprises, how to industrialize in the absence of mutual confidence, governmental competence, skilled work-

ers, capital accumulation, and a social stigma on short finger-
nails. These continue to be relevant questions to irrelevant
exhortations to sluggish, corrupt, undisciplined, and impoverished societies that they get their countries moving
and revolutionize themselves after the example of our life,
achievement, and dreams.

Another lesson is that people even of the same race can
vary tremendously in national personality, as did the Chinese and the Japanese. Programming and projecting the
U.S.A. may, because of differing character, outlook, and
energy in the recipients, influence Country X in one direction, Country Y in another, and Country Z scarcely at all.
The number of differing reactions will correspond to the
number of "target" countries.

To inspire a nation by our life, achievements, and dreams
to the degree that it modernizes itself does not guarantee
that it will thereby be converted to a live-and-let-live policy
in its international relations. It may elect a contrary course
and turn on us. Or it may go its own self-assertive way without respect to us or the UN Charter.

Turning more particularly to our present battle for men's
minds, the conditions of the conflict are not entirely favorable to us. Much is made of reservoirs of goodwill for the
United States. This is true, for such reservoirs do exist. But
it is also true that a characteristic of many reservoirs is that
they are dammed up. A pervasive unsympathy for us holds
back the natural flow of such goodwill as may exist.

The unsympathy varies from petty irritations to unrea-
soning hostility. Even the people nearest to us, our next-
door neighbors, speaking the same language and sharing

pretty much the same origins and culture—the Canadians—are somewhat less than uncritical of us. There is so much of us, we intrude upon them, and we have long taken them for granted.

The quality of the wet sheepdog in the parlor, demonstrative, well disposed, sniffing everyone, into everything, likewise irritates our European friends. They are grateful to us, of course, as a watchdog. But when we tug at their sleeves to go out and hunt Castros with us, the familiar human reaction is: "Don't be a nuisance, go chase your own Cubans."

More serious is the anti-Americanism in the underdeveloped countries this side of the Curtain. For the underdeveloped peoples, the primitive force of race—racial suspicions, resentments, and hatreds—may prove to be stronger than ideology. It is generations deep in the passions of Asia and Africa. It is not absent among the nonwhites of Latin America. That we are predominantly white is sufficient to aggravate the fester of nationalism, to find indignant self-virtue in every publicized act of segregation or violence against the American Negro, and to inflate and nurture insults, as visitors to our shores, in encounters with sorely beset New York policemen, hotel receptionists, gentlemen's clubs, and Howard Johnson hostesses.

Race is also the fuel of ideology. Anti-imperialism is felt with fervor long after its weight has been lifted, not simply because of distant political or economic relationships but more likely because of past or present personal humiliations by white men.

The same holds true of communism. Its appeal among underdeveloped peoples is stimulated by racial grudges. This is because Marxism-Leninism is not only militantly anti-imperialist but is also loud in its protestations for racial equality. Largely overlooked is Russian light pigmentation, extensive racial prejudices in the U.S.S.R., and Soviet imperialism from Mongolia through Central Asia to East Germany.

That the Russians are white is not, however, entirely disregarded. Primitive color prejudice exists between the Russians and the Chinese, a common ideology notwithstanding. The Chinese have sought to exploit this elemental antipathy among other nonwhite Communists, to the Kremlin's intense indignation, trying to turn them against Moscow and into alignment with Peking, which pretends to be the capital of colored communism.

The white man's whiteness is not his sole burden nowadays in treating with underdeveloped nations. In our case we also encounter the natural envy of the poor. We are the richest of the rich nations, and in our bounty we have bestowed benefits upon the poor countries with unprecedented liberality. This is the cause of an embarrassed beholdingness, inverted into resentment, in the proud. In those of a practical bent, the embarrassment is soon quelled by rising expectations of continuing benefits as an accustomed due. A lessening of the benefits naturally produces a sense of being unjustly deprived of what has become a right.

American intervention, before we became the Good Neighbor, left in Latin-American memories that have not died out, an apprehension of United States power cracking down on them. That we have been for over thirty years bland as mother's milk, and more freely flowing, matters little. Yanqui imperialism remains a specter in the Latin mind.

Being white, rich, and reformed imperialists makes for something of a propaganda handicap. What do we do about foreign antipathy?

Possibly the first thing to do is to stop being so agitated about it.

We might with profit consider a predecessor in pre-eminent power, the British. No one liked the British much. For their part, they recognized foreign dislike for its worth, including the valid criticism therein. But they did not become obsessed by unpopularity. Nor did they waste energy in vainly combatting those international neuroses that were curable only by (if even by that) Britain's disappearance from the face of the earth.

What was usually taken for British arrogance was merely British boredom. Generations of Britons had learned the futility of explaining to alien minds the rationale of world-wide power and its attendant responsibilities.

But ours is another temperament. However composed we may become, whatever aplomb we may muster, we feel the necessity of reacting to the ideological offensive of the Communists. We cannot simply ignore pervasive and persistent thought-aggression throughout the world, damaging to our interests.

So, as a government, we react. The fact that in a generally unsympathetic world situation our government does react is in contrast to the missionary movement. Christian proselytization was spontaneous; it was on the offensive. Our agitated opinion-forming is not spontaneous. It is a defensive reflex, a response to Soviet ideological aggression. Were it not for the communist menace, we would scarcely have embarked on this, unnatural for us, proselytization of foreigners by the Federal bureaucracy and circulating celebrities.

With the Communists on the offensive and with us on the defensive, the battle for men's minds is snarled in a double paradox. To the bewildered foreigner serious enough to make a try at sorting out the issues, our identifiable outlook is in apparent conflict: (*a*) the Christian ethic of political principles enunciated by the founders of the Republic and (*b*) the materialistic, hedonistic philosophy produced by our industrial and merchandising genius.

The second paradox derives from the ideological confrontation between us and the Communists. Our case is publicly stated on alternative (*a*): we represent the spiritual, idealistic, humanistic values. We consider them, "the splendor of our ideals," to be revolutionary in their impact on the unconverted. The communist dogma is aggressively materialistic. Yet our attraction for foreigners is our superlatively successful materialism, "our wealth or power," the level of which it is the communist ideal to equal and overtake. Perversely, the communist magnetism for the underdeveloped peoples is ideas, theory, and, save the mark, idealism—else there would be no communist fanaticism, which is a perversion of idealism.

Our mosaic of traditional beliefs, the totality of which we call democracy, has relevance and deeply treasured significance for us. But for others, American democracy is particularly American, remote, and inapplicable to themselves. As for the lessons of the American Revolution, they seem academic to the Asian, African, or Latin American, having little bearing on the extremity in which he finds himself.

The American Revolution is in time, magnitude, and intensity far distant from what goes on in modern revolutionary situations—from the October Revolution in Russia, to the long-drawn-out upheaval in China, to the feverish frustrations of Arab socialism in North Africa and the Near East, and to the machete Marxist performance in Brazil. It is the difference between an uprising commanded by disaffected gentry and a desperate, groping, ignorant compulsion among those who feel their only hope is to overturn and smash not only the old regime but the whole social order and to replace it with almost any blatant denial of what they live under, almost any sort of plebeian dispensation.

The American Revolution was essentially conservative. The revolutions of the underdeveloped countries are metamorphic, boundless in impulse to wreck and make over. As such they present an exciting opportunity to power-hungry schemers, those who, as Hamilton observed, begin "their career by paying an obsequious court to the people, commencing demagogues and ending tyrants."

What Jefferson and Patrick Henry had to say about liberty and the pursuit of happiness was regarded as worthily revolutionary by the educated minority in underdeveloped countries when they, too, were colonials, but now that they are sovereign, the revolutionary oligarchies view such sentiments as counterrevolutionary.

In contrast, the combination of American materialism and

American pop culture is one of the most potent influences ever loosed on the world. The appeal is nearly universal because merchandising creativity, research, and development meant it to be so. The infinite permutations of plastics, luminescence, frigidity, moving metal parts, heat, extrusions, electrical impulses, petrochemical fibers, swoosh of air in and swish of air out, artificial flavors, sonic effects, and liquid concentrates diluted outdo the total philosophical and moral output of our Founding Fathers. "This," simple people everywhere sigh and say, "ah, this is America."

And if for lack of cash the foreigner cannot buy such tangible bliss on earth, we offer to rich and poor alike everyman's effortless Nirvana: on film, tape, radio, and TV and in McCallism-Playboyism. This is our immaterial thrust, our un-ideology, the power of which we fail to appreciate.

Some Americans are ashamed of the success abroad of this neopubescent way of life. It is not putting our best foot forward. That is true. But there it is. And it must be admitted that the message is comprehensible to all and appallingly popular with most.

The utilitarian, the vapid and the vulgar of our life, achievements and dreams homogenize into a successful revolutionary export. A measure of the revolutionary success is that the communist rulers regard the blend as a distracting and subversive influence which, if allowed free entry, would undermine Marxism-Leninism. This is one of the main reasons for the Iron Curtain.

Being an open society, Western Europe is succumbing to this revolution of flatulence. The appeal is relevant, and with Europe's growing affluence the revolutionary goals are attainable by almost everyone. Quality and taste are fighting a counterrevolutionary rearguard action. But the odds are against them.

With the underdeveloped countries it is yet another story. The materialistic appeal of the Miami Beach blend is there, but it is usually not relevant because it is, for most, unattainable. It excites revolutionary impulses that need money to be satisfied. Poverty thwarts fulfillment. The pop culture stimulates the rising expectations with dreams of possessing that which, upon confrontation with reality, is priced beyond possession.

The result of this revolutionary force on the emergent poor is resentful frustration, heightening the basic discontent of poverty. From there it is but a step to a will to revolt and receptivity to any plausible scheme of violent revolution. This is where communism, in theory and insurrectionary technique, appears to be relevant to backward peoples, not because they like Russians or Chinese or want to be ruled by them. Quite the contrary. It is because many of them are drawn to authority, purpose, mass solidarity, violent revolt, a shared formula for self-realization, the government's taking problems off their shoulders and promises of security in a utopian collective society. The less enured to choice and decision a people, the more attractive this simplifying formula.

The practical aspirant to power in the underdeveloped countries tends toward the totalitarian choice because— quite aside from the agreeable coincidence that he, the government, and the "people" might merge into one, with him as the father of the trinity—he recognizes that his people are not equal to what we understand by democracy. And the people themselves, after colonial rule, submission to native tyrants, or "governing themselves" through scalawags and weaklings, are receptive to totalitarianism in which the simple man finds spurious realization as an individual in local party meetings, "popular" demonstrations, and possession of a militiaman's gun, while actually losing his individuality in the socially secured people.

This is what happened in Cuba. And in Cuba, as elsewhere under Communist tyranny, the people soon found themselves betrayed by what was purported to be their revolution.

And yet, since mid-century, the spread of communism as a projection of Soviet power in the world has not been extensive.

One of the three facets of communism, its technique of insurrection, has been less than wholly successful since the Chinese revolution. The technique was effective in Cuba and partially so in Indochina. In Greece, Iran, the Philippines, and Malaya the uprisings failed. In the future, communist insurrections may succeed in some Latin-American countries.

There is a second facet of communism—ideology in its fundamentalist Marxist-Leninist expression—but it has not gained significant ground. Communism as an infallible unitary doctrine has been fragmented by the Russo-Chinese quarrel and the growth of polycentrism. Communist ideology has been borrowed from in dilutions and unlikely admixtures by some of the new states in Asia and Africa. The Marxist-Islamic brew in some sub-Saharan nations of Africa is an example. And nationalist variants of communism may come to power through democratic elections in a few Latin American countries.

Another facet, the communist system of domination and rule, has been more extensively drawn upon, but also in diffused form. This is so, not necessarily because the revolutionary oligarchies were tender of heart, but because of a pervasive temperamental disarray. The one-party Afro-socialist dictatorship of the immortal Osagyefo Kwame Nkrumah is a case in point. Nevertheless, species of authoritarianism derived from Leninism will probably be the most enduring legacy of communism in the underdeveloped states, with eventually little or no allegiance to its originators.

Rampant nationalism in the underdeveloped nations, particularly the new ones, has been the strongest antibody to the extension of Soviet authority and power. Backward governments have accepted from the Communists, Russian and Chinese, insurrectionary techniques, ideology, and totalitarian systems, but always with reservations and modifications. It is, of course, a dangerous game. If the emergent nation becomes dependent upon Moscow or Peking, as Cuba in its selfmade chaos did, the risk is great of penetration of control mechanisms and take-over. If this happens, the country becomes an adjunct of Soviet or Chinese power. Otherwise the power advantages to Moscow or Peking are conditional, most obviously with respect to the economic cost of trying to maintain control.

While ideology is a mishmash in the backward countries, in the rest of the world it is obsolescent. This is most evident in Western Europe, its breeding ground, from whence emerged Marxism, nazism, and fascism, for Western Europe was to ideologies what the Near and Middle East were to religions. Notwithstanding the popularity of socialism, ideology is passé in Western Europe because it has been made largely irrelevant by the orderly adoption of many moderate socialist principles, the success of the Marshall Plan, and a consequent social equilibrium. The only possible revival of rampant ideology would seem to be in the event that Western Europe suffers a prolonged depression.

As for the communist countries, ideology is kept nominally alive by the system of domination, including isolation, and by rote. People have lived before on what had ceased to have fresh and vital meaning to them, so long as the familiar outward forms and structures remained. With time, the rub of internal and external contradictions will erode even the system encasing the people.

The truth is that our battle for men's minds in the past decade has gone much better than we have anxiously imagined. The principal reason is that communism has done poorly for Moscow and Peking, largely as a result of their own economic botches and of the vigor of nationalism in the new countries, the old countries, and in the communist camp itself.

The industrialized countries of the West have, in contrast, flourished beyond expectation and become a symbol of success. This does not of course provide an answer in the minds of the underdeveloped peoples to their own problems. They want to get where we are without going through a slow growth process. But the contrast between the Communists and the West has raised doubts about blind adherence to Marxism.

Obviously some of what we are trying to do in opinion-forming is futile. Some of it is silly. And some is even damaging. Foreigners, like us, are stubborn folk, not much moved by alien exhortation unless it suits their book. What we have to say about ourselves is rarely assimilable by others, even when understood. What we offer is, in part, taken; what is learned may be used against us—as what is taken from our enemy may be used against him. What we deem ordinary and even shoddy is admired and pathetically emulated. What we cherish is spurned.

We are preoccupied with ideology. We fail to distinguish between hostile ideology associated with power, which is a real threat, and hostile ideology without significant power, which is impotent enmity.

More significantly, we are insufficiently aware that civilization is moving out of the epoch of political philosophies and entering the era of know-how, with us in the vanguard.

Should the lagging countries move forward and not sink into a bog of squalor and chaos, it will be mainly because administrative and technical know-how is applied. It will not be because of ideology—or even the adoption of universal suffrage and a bicameral legislature. And if the Communists are to sober from their doctrinal hallucinations, it will be because the pragmatic possessors of know-how—the only element capable of bringing the communist countries up from their material inferiority—wear down the fanatics.

Our approach to the so-called battle for men's minds should be more relaxed and modest. It should be more modest in claims of what our life, achievements, and dreams can do for others in an uncertain world. It should be more modest in the scope of "programs" undertaken, the size of staffs engaged therein, and the number of gallivanting political celebrities roaming the face of the earth creating what Dr. Daniel J. Boorstin calls pseudo-events. And rather than expostulating—in effect to ourselves without meaning to our auditors—we would more often better be silent.

Most important of all, it is not what we say abroad that is vital. Our first obligation is to ourselves, that at home we fulfill in integrity our native heritage and promise, that we be the ruler of our own spirit.